P9-DOF-175

Praise for

150 Most-Asked Questions About
Midlife Sex, Love, and Intimacy

"Ruth Jacobowitz's *150 Most-Asked Questions About Midlife Sex, Love, and Intimacy* was researched and written to enlighten and liberate the reader from the myths and misinformation our culture brings to adult sexuality, passion, and love. So read, communicate with your partner, and enjoy!"

—June M. Reinisch, Ph.D.
Director Emerita, The Kinsey
Institute for Research in Sex,
Gender, and Reproduction

"The empowerment of women to make informed medical choices is the goal of The National Council on Women's Health, which believes this book to offer an important addition in decision-making for the midlife woman. Ruth Jacobowitz is to be praised for listening and responding to the questions of women. There are many approaches to achieving a more fulfilling sexual relationship but education is the basis of all of these choices. Her attention to issues of concern such as hormone replacement, as well as improved partner communication and good exercise and nutrition are to be commended. The author has made available to her reader a comprehensive listing of resources. It is a pleasure to recommend this book."

—JEAN L. FOURCROY, M.D., PH.D.
President-elect, American Medical Women's Association
Past President, National Council on Women's Health

"Straightforward answers to questions you should ask about midlife love life."

—ROBERT N. BUTLER, M.D.
Professor of Geriatrics, Mount Sinai School of Medicine;
Co-author, *Love and Sex After 60*

"This book is a continuation of Ruth Jacobowitz's quest to educate women to get involved with the management of their own health care and well-being. It will open many new doors for many women who have experienced decreased energy, libido, and sense of well-being and increased headaches and dry skin during the perimenopausal and menopausal years. Ruth Jacobowitz's sensitivity to women's needs is obvious from her personal interviews as these women talk freely about important but private issues."

—M. E. TED QUIGLEY, M.D., FRCS (C) FACOG
Clinical Associate Professor, Departments of Reproductive Medicine and Community and Family Medicine, UCSD School of Medicine; Director of Research at the Mary Birch Hospital for Women, Sharp Memorial Hospital in San Diego

"Ruth Jacobowitz's book is valuable! It should be read by men as well as women. Many of the conflicts between the sexes could be solved if we understood each others' physiology. You should read this book. It could solve a lot of problems."

—ESTELLE R. RAMEY, M.D., PH.D.
Professor Emeritus, Georgetown University
School of Medicine

"With characteristic energy, enthusiasm, practicality, and optimism, Ruth Jacobowitz has once again brought to the general public a useful synthesis of medical opinion about the vital but neglected subject of women's sexual desire in the last half of life. Thank you!"

—STEPHEN B. LEVINE, M.D.
Clinical Professor of Psychiatry at Case Western
Reserve University School of Medicine;
Co-Director, Center for Marital and Sexual Health;
Author, *Sex Is Not Simple* and *Sexual Life: A Clinician's Guide*

150

Most-Asked

Questions

About

Midlife Sex,

Love, and

Intimacy

Also by Ruth S. Jacobowitz

150 Most-Asked Questions About Osteoporosis

150 Most-Asked Questions About Menopause

Managing Your Menopause
(with Wulf Utian, M.D., Ph.D.)

150
Most-Asked
Questions
About
Midlife Sex,
Love, and
Intimacy

*What Women and Their Partners
Really Want to Know*

Ruth S. Jacobowitz

HEARST BOOKS NEW YORK

NEW HANOVER COUNTY
PUBLIC LIBRARY
201 CHESTNUT STREET
WILMINGTON, NC 28401

Copyright © 1995 by Ruth S. Jacobowitz

The ideas, suggestions, and answers to questions in this book are not intended to substitute for the help and services of a trained health professional. All matters regarding your health require medical consultation and supervision. Answers to questions concerning your individual needs require consultation with a qualified professional on questions specific to your care to assure that your unique situation has been evaluated and so that the choices of care or treatment are appropriate for you, the reader.

The names of people and cities referred to in the anecdotes in this book have been changed to protect the identities of the individuals concerned.

All rights reserved. No part of this book may be reproduced or utilized in any form or by any means, electronic or mechanical, including photocopying, recording, or by any information storage or retrieval system, without permission in writing from the Publisher. Inquiries should be addressed to Permissions Department, William Morrow and Company, Inc., 1350 Avenue of the Americas, New York, N.Y. 10019.

It is the policy of William Morrow and Company, Inc., and its imprints and affiliates, recognizing the importance of preserving what has been written, to print the books we publish on acid-free paper, and we exert our best efforts to that end.

Library of Congress Cataloging-in-Publication Data

Jacobowitz, Ruth S.

150 most-asked questions about midlife sex, love, and intimacy : what women and their partners really want to know / Ruth S. Jacobowitz.

p. cm.

Includes bibliographical references and index.

ISBN 0-688-12890-4

1. Middle aged women—Sexual behavior. 2. Sex. I. Title. II. Title: One hundred fifty most-asked questions about midlife sex, love, and intimacy. III. Title: One hundred and fifty most-asked questions about midlife sex, love and intimacy.

HQ1059.4.J33   1995

306.77′084′4—dc20   94-3465

CIP

Printed in the United States of America

First Edition

1 2 3 4 5 6 7 8 9 10

BOOK DESIGN BY BRIAN MULLIGAN

For Paul, my husband, lover, and best friend and
For my closest friends—our daughters, Jan, Jody,
and Julie—who are great wives and mothers all

foreword

IF YOU HAVE SAILED by your fortieth or fiftieth birthday a number of years ago, perhaps, like me, you've
looked in the mirror and said to yourself, "I'm still just
a twenty-year-old inside—who in the world is that
mature person looking back at me?" It has always been
my view that you ARE that younger person. It's the
mirror, our society, the media, and probably some
images from your own past that are sending false
messages.

Are we doomed to wander lost through a dimly defined land called middle age? And if at times we are
confused about how old we really are and how old we
really should be thinking and acting, particularly when
it comes to sex, none of us is alone in this state of
mind. Unfortunately, to that confusion is often linked

understandable but needless stress on ourselves and on our relationships.

Why in this day and at our age should we be entangled in a new sexual mystery that seems to match some of the same uncertainties we felt when it all began in adolescence? After all, our society was supposed to have undergone a "sexual revolution" in recent decades. Talk shows, movies, and magazines are filled with discussions of this kind or that kind of sex. Mostly of "that kind"—sexual behavior which is unusual, not part of the repertoire of most people. No wonder so many people, of all ages, are looking for accurate, factual information about sexuality.

Ask yourself this simple question: When was the last time you saw a movie or prime-time television show in which mature partners were clearly turned on to each other and were passionately enjoying their sexual relationship? If you saw it at all, it was likely a sitcom and the couple were the butt of all kinds of jokes and embarrassed innuendo. And what's more, the couple, or at least the woman, was probably portrayed as embarrassed by the whole business. Of course, middle-aged men are seen in erotic situations with much younger women all the time. That's an accepted tradition in our and many other cultures. But more mature and older women are rarely portrayed as passionately enraptured and happy about being in such a state.

One can't help but wonder just who it is that is really embarrassed by the sexuality of people who are not playing beach volleyball, not swaggering or slinking around in skin-tight jeans with bare chests or midriffs, and not into heavy metal or rap music. Is it the youth-obsessed advertisers or the young creative artists themselves who literally can't imagine what it's like to be past forty, let alone have a sex life at that age? Are there still some people out there who cannot believe that Mom and Dad, those ancient adults, really had, and are having sex, other than for procreation?

The truth is that no matter who is responsible for the false image of passion evaporating in a sexual desert of middle age, sex is, can be, and should be alive and well throughout our lives. But even in these supposedly enlightened times, dismal distortions of human nature remain. This situation is particularly disturbing as our population shifts toward a greater proportion of people over the age of forty. The myth of being over-the-sexual-hill by then robs vast numbers of people of one of life's most significant, enriching, and healthy pleasures during the second half of life.

The mistaken notion of the death of passion was finally laid to rest for me during the nine years I wrote a syndicated newspaper column. During those years I received a surprising number of letters from men and women in their sixties, seventies, eighties, and even nineties who were confused or frightened by finding themselves passionately in love—sometimes for the first time in their lives after the loss of a dearly beloved spouse with whom they had never shared sexual passion. These older individuals couldn't believe or understand what was happening to them. There were no models, no media personalities, no stories or self-help books for them to consult. Some even asked if there was a medicine they could have prescribed which would "cure" their feelings and desires. There were others, however, who wanted advice on how to get their bodies back into working order after years of disuse and neglect so that they could enjoy their new-found relationship to the fullest.

It is clear that the fantasies and experiences of adolescence and young adulthood need to give way to a revised but not necessarily diminished view of passion and sexual pleasure later in life. This new view, I might add, wouldn't do young people any harm to consider and incorporate as well.

With a variety of increasingly well tuned hormone treatments more generally available, many of the physical problems that beset our grandmothers need not be obstacles for the vast majority of women today. If we can break free from the genitally focused, intercourse-demanding sexuality of our often mythical youth, we can open ourselves to the many different forms of sexual pleasure that are available to us. Everything from cuddling to cunnilingus, from fondling to fellatio, and from massage to masturbation are there for our pleasure throughout our lives.

But the possibilities remain only that, unless we are able to see ourselves and our partners as not really different from the youths looking out at us in the mirror. For these possibilities to be realized, two key elements are required: accurate knowledge—the truth—and the readiness to communicate your feelings, your desires, and your pleasures to your partner. For example, many adults don't know that research has revealed most women, at any age, do not experience orgasm from penile thrusting alone—clitoral stimulation before or during intercourse is necessary; that erection, orgasm, and ejaculation are separate physiological functions in men and therefore a man can have a satisfying orgasm without being erect; that masturbation can actually help postmenopausal women without partners to maintain genital and urinary tract health for themselves and for the happy circumstance of falling in love with a future partner.

Information of this kind can make an enormous difference in the pleasure, joy, and communication of love for one's lifetime. Ignorance of these facts can cause pain, unhappiness, and loneliness.

This book provides the information needed and will

help you to discover and incorporate the language with which to think and talk about an enriched sense of yourself and your sexuality. Based on extensive interviews with women who can remember the day that Kennedy was killed, Ruth Jacobowitz speaks directly to the women and men of several generations about their most significant sexual concerns. Whether your questions lie in the realms of health or physiology or those concerned with your feelings and sexual performance, you and your partner will find this book a comforting, supportive, and informative guide to the sexual life you deserve and can enjoy for the next twenty, thirty, forty, or fifty years.

Ruth Jacobowitz's *150 Most-Asked Questions About Midlife Sex, Love, and Intimacy* was researched and written to enlighten and liberate the reader from the myths and misinformation our culture brings to adult sexuality, passion, and love. So read, communicate with your partner, and enjoy!

—June Machover Reinisch, Ph.D.
Director Emerita
The Kinsey Institute for Research
in Sex, Gender, and Reproduction

Acknowledgments

THIS BOOK WAS WRITTEN in honor of and at the request of the women and men I met as I lectured around the country on women's midlife health issues, as well as those who wrote to me or telephoned with comment, question, and compliment. It could not have been written without the input of each person who came to hear me speak or just to meet me at a bookstore and who took the time to ask questions, fill out my questionnaires, and share their personal stories with me. This book could not have been researched so thoroughly without the help of many physicians, psychologists, therapists, and counselors who gave unstintingly of their time and expertise to help me.

In the past several years I have crisscrossed the nation many, many times, either on tour with my books or speaking at book fairs, bookstores, and at women's health seminars sponsored by many prestigious medical organizations as an expression of their continuing commitment to consumer education. I am deeply appreciative of that sponsorship and support.

I am also grateful to the physicians who generously shared the podium and medical information with me over the years: Mary K. Beard, M.D.; Sarah Berga, M.D.; Robert Bury, M.D.; Wendy Buchi, M.D.; Charles Chesnut, M.D.; Maureen Dudgeon, M.D.; Gloria Halverson, M.D.; Peter Hickox, M.D.; Howard Judd, M.D.; Deborah Nemiro, M.D.; Zachariah Newton, M.D.; Jon S. Nielsen, M.D.; Roger D. Matthews, M.D.; Elizabeth McClure, M.D.; M. E. Ted Quigley, M.D.; William D. Schlaff, M.D.; Sheldon Weinstein, M.D.; and Neil Wolfson, M.D.

The most in-depth interviews for this book were held with Drs. Estelle Ramey, June M. Reinisch, M. E. Ted Quigley, Robert Butler, and with the professional staff at Cleveland's Center for Marital and Sexual Health: Drs. Stephen B. Levine, Stanley E. Althof, Ellen A. Rosenblatt, and Elizabeth B. Stern, and with Candace B. Risen, L.I.S.W. My appreciation to them is unbounded.

More than 1500 women filled out my sex, love, and intimacy questionnaire and added whatever other personal information they wished. Those questionnaires are invaluable. I interviewed more than one hundred women at length for this book and you will find their stories throughout. Their names have been changed and I must thank them in the anonymity that I promised them. Each of you will find yourselves in the text, perhaps in a different city, with a changed career, or with an altered age or physical description, but you will know who you are. You must know how grateful I am that you trusted me enough to bare your souls so that others might find within this work satisfactory routes for successful transitions for themselves. That kind of trust is no small matter and I thank you. I also thank the women who met with me repeatedly in small group discussions. I know it is even harder to share such closely held personal information in a group, but we all grew together in the synergy of sharing and trusting.

I would like to thank my editor, Toni Sciarra, for her help with this project. I must thank family members as well. My sisters and brothers Harriet and Bud Lewis, Susan and Leonard Rosenberg, Rifkie and Bill Jacobowitz, and Max Jacobowitz continue to show sincere interest and pride in my work. To my other family members and to my friends, I am grateful for your interest and for your understanding of my self-imposed, sometimes crazy schedule.

My understanding and proud children must be

thanked profusely. Their pride in me nurtures me every day of my life. So, thanks to my kids: Jan Jacobowitz, her husband, Alvin, and sons Jeffrey Asher (who pitched in to help) and Ryan Jeremy Lodish; Jody, David, Claire Michelle, and Jake Cremer Austin; and Julie (who helped me with the editing process), Lowell, Michael Aaron, Cara Elizabeth, and Danielle Alexa Potiker. You're quite simply the best cheerleaders and I love you for it.

Last, and first, and always to Paul, my husband of more than forty years, my undying gratitude. You not only survived my youth, but you thrive with me in this magical midlife time when I finally learned that I could love you unstintingly, because I now have the time and mind to love myself as well. It's the midlife gift!

—Ruth S. Jacobowitz

Contents

Foreword by June Machover
Reinisch, Ph.D.   *vii*

Acknowledgments   *xiii*

A Special Note   *xix*

Before You Begin This Book   *xxi*

1   This Is Not Your Usual Book About Sex!   *1*

2   What Is the Role of Sexuality at Midlife?   *31*

3   How Do Hormones Affect
    Our Sexual Selves?   *58*

4   How Do I Avoid Sexual Boredom?   *78*

5   What Can I Do to Increase
    My Interest in Sex?   *94*

6   What Are Some Routes to Sexual Arousal?   *113*

7   Why Don't We Just Talk About It?
    Improving Sexual Communication   *129*

| 8 | *How Do I Get My Sexual Affairs in Order?* | *150* |

| 9 | *What Can I Do to Maintain Sexual Sensation?* | *166* |

| 10 | *What Are Good Sex Signals?* | *182* |

| 11 | *How Do I Gain Sexual Energy Through Exercise?* | *192* |

| 12 | *What Is a Good Sex Diet?* | *204* |

| 13 | *How Do I Fulfill My Sexual Needs When I'm Flying Solo?* | *217* |

| 14 | *What Are Good Midlife Sexual Ethics and Politics?* | *227* |

| 15 | *Why Don't Our Doctors Talk to Us About Our Sex Lives and Where Can I Go for Help?* | *240* |

| 16 | *What Is the Real Meaning of Intimacy?* | *252* |

| | *A Final Note: Write to Me, Talk to Me* | *260* |

| | *Appendices* | *263* |

| | *Index* | *289* |

| | *About the Author* | *305* |

A Special Note

For your ease in reading and in finding the answers to your questions, I have chosen not to interrupt our question-and-answer period with a full explanation of how our sex hormones work with each mention of the role our sex hormones—both female and male—play in our sex lives. For information and easy reference, I have placed an important section called "The Anatomy of Sex" at the beginning of Chapter 2. With an understanding of how these hormones work, combined with the sound information contained in this book, I believe that the path to the treasure of midlife sex, love, and intimacy will be easy to find and to follow.

Before You Begin
This Book

I was deeply engrossed in an article I was reading when the voice on the television set summoned me. Suddenly, there was Germaine Greer being interviewed on ABC's *Prime Time Live.* Germaine Greer, one of the most outspoken of the feminists, wore a simple plaid cotton dress. She looked plain and loose, with no apparent benefit of cosmetics, with no apparent support of undergarments. Her short hair looked not styled, but rather chopped off. There was still that searing fire in her eyes that I remembered from seeing her speak in the early years of the feminist movement, and her manner was frank and forthright. Germaine Greer, icon of my younger years, iconoclastic and outrageous still, was describing *The Change,* the title of her book and, as she explained, of her new stage of life.

There was little doubt that Greer had taken charge of the interview, which was being held at her home in Great Britain. "Getting laid at this time of life is much too difficult," she was saying when my attention was grabbed by the interview. "Give it up," she said "and tend to your geese." As she spoke, she led her interviewer into the barnyard, where she deliberately scattered food for her flock.

That was the moment that my attention became riveted to "the change" and sex. Was it true that we had to abandon sex—a basic activity of life to which many of us loved to abandon ourselves? I thought not.

I had always detested that euphemism for menopause—"the change of life." At midlife, I didn't want my life to change—certainly not my sex life. It was at that moment that I knew that sex, love, and intimacy at midlife and beyond would be the subject of my next survey and of this book.

During the next year and a half, I began to distribute survey questionnaires to women all over the country. I had carefully, painstakingly decided what I wanted and needed to know. I needed to know whether Germaine Greer was right. I wanted to know from the women how their interest in sex had fared in their middle years; if it had changed, I wanted to learn how they felt about the change. I also wanted to know what their marital status was, what was important to them in a relationship, how their partner handled any change in their sex life, whether they were premenopausal, menopausal, or postmenopausal, their age, and whether they were interested in finding out how to increase their interest in sex and to stimulate their sexual satisfaction. I learned a lot.

I also interviewed couples and a number of women—all in differing stages of their midlife sex lives—who agreed to meet and to talk openly about sex, love, and intimacy. And I interviewed experts in the fields of psychiatry, psychology, marital therapy, geriatrics, endocrinology, and human sexuality. This book is the result of what I learned.

Little did I know, as I began my survey, that I would very soon meet, indeed have dinner with, Germaine Greer along with a group of other women, all unknown to me at that time.

We met on the occasion of my first attendance at a meeting of the International Menopause Society in Stockholm, Sweden. Greer was also in Stockholm for the International Menopause meeting. A dinner was arranged for sixteen of us—all women—to meet her.

After dinner, I introduced myself to Germaine Greer and asked her if she meant what she said about sex on *Prime Time Live.*

She had meant it all, she insisted. Greer explained in her no-nonsense way that she found that at this time of life, sex quite simply did not interest her at all, and she had discovered that she didn't mind one bit. She added mischievously that she had not given up sex, but rather that it had given her up. Nonetheless, the result was the same. Imagine this confession from the former sex-kitten mistress of the late genius Italian film director Federico Fellini, and of sexy and beautiful movie actor Warren Beatty, among others! (Greer discussed these relationships in a candid interview in *Mirabella* magazine when her book was published.)

Once, in the earliest days of her change, she admitted to "enduring" a testosterone shot to reverse her lack of interest in sex. "I hated the result," she said. "I felt that my clitoris had taken control of my life and that all I was doing was searching for sex, sex, sex." If this was what testosterone does, perhaps this testosterone rush was why, she posited, men masturbate in shop windows all over Europe.

There is no question: Germaine Greer is outspoken, even outlandish and outrageous. I felt an instant fondness for her. I felt an instant kinship with her. At the end of the evening, she signed for me the outsized souvenir postcard of the Ulla Windblahd Restaurant where we had dined. She wrote "For Ruth, with love, Germaine Greer." Between the words "with love" and her signature, she drew a heart. The heart, shaped like a uterus perhaps, has two squiggly lines emerging from either side of the top, ending in nothing. I speculate whether these represent our Fallopian tubes with the ovaries missing, having shriveled at menopause and then disappeared.

I felt fortunate to have met Greer, but I offer this book in opposition to her charge that at midlife we should give up sex and tend our geese. Rather, I think we should take charge of our good health and continue to have good sex if we want it! For some of us that may mean acquiring a new lover; however, for many of us it will mean learning how to reignite the fire in our own long-term relationship and create that sense of mystery, danger, and novelty that is inherent in a sexual affair. It is well worth the effort!

150
Most-Asked
Questions
About
Midlife Sex,
Love, and
Intimacy

CHAPTER I

This Is Not Your Usual Book About Sex!

THIS BOOK IS UNIQUE. It is neither Freudian nor Jungian. It is not Erica Jongian. This book contains the 150 most-asked questions about midlife sex, love, and intimacy gathered from thousands of woman and the carefully researched answers to those questions. It shares the contents of interviews that I conducted with women about their sex lives at midlife and later, but not their identities. It is explicit in detailing their desires and their disappointments, their pleasure and their pain, their sexual needs and their search for solutions, just as they related them to me.

One of the strengths of this book is that it is written by a medical journalist and a former hospital administrator. It is important, I think, that I do not work in the fields that impact these subjects, but rather that this is a woman-to-woman book, written without medical jargon or medical dogma or bias, although many experts were consulted and gave freely of their time and expertise.

The foundation of this book is built from many materials. Following as it does my first two books in this series, *150 Most-Asked Questions About Menopause* and *150 Most-Asked Questions About Osteoporosis,* both published in 1993, it incorporates the results from fifteen thousand questionnaires and hundreds of written questions from the women who attended the seminars and programs in which I have participated over the past four years. These questionnaires all included questions about changes in sexual desire and about pain with intercourse caused by thinning and drying of vaginal tissue.

It also includes responses from fifteen hundred new questionnaires that dealt specifically with questions about midlife sex, love, and intimacy gathered from women who attended the programs held during 1992, 1993, and 1994.

To broaden my base of respondents, a number of menopause support-group leaders around the country kindly agreed to distribute the survey to their members.

The editors of "Midlife Woman," an excellent women's newsletter published in Minneapolis by Sharon

Slattehaugh and Carole Moore, helped by running a notice in their publication to inform their readers nationwide of the availability of the sex questionnaire. (Information about "Midlife Woman" can be found in Appendix D, as can information about "A Friend Indeed," "Menopause News," and "Sex After Forty," excellent newsletters for women in the prime of life. *Éternelle,* a new magazine devoted to the midlife woman, is also listed there.)

Other vital data came from the firsthand experiences of the women who joined my discussion groups on these subjects in several cities, from women I interviewed in person or by phone, and from the experiences and comments of the women who have called or written to me since my previous books were published.

From all of these varied and valuable sources, I have compiled the one hundred and fifty most-asked questions about midlife sex, love, and intimacy contained in this book. When I shared the title of this book with Mike, my personal trainer, a beefy and bright young man in his late twenties, he asked, "Ruth, when exactly is this midlife you're always talking about?" I answered quickly while pumping iron, "Mike, it's always ten years older than I am!"

The number-one question I had as I began my research for this book was whether painful intercourse was the sole determinant of lack of sexual desire, or whether diminished testosterone levels, psychological or physical changes, or simply the lack of a partner were reasons why some women report having no interest in sex.

Let's set the hormone record straight. We women all have our share of the male hormone testosterone and it is the hormone that triggers sexual desire in both men and women. So, is painful intercourse caused by a lack of the female sex hormone estrogen (and the subsequent thinning and drying of the vaginal canal)? Do low testosterone levels cause some women to have no interest in sex? Do *both* factors create problems? And if it can be both, which comes first? Does it always occur first? Are there other factors at work?

There is so little definitive medical research performed on this confounding subject that after reviewing the medical literature and after talking with many experts—physicians, psychiatrists, clinical psychologists, sexologists, and a knowledgeable registered nurse who, having rejected allopathic medicine, works primarily with homeopathy—I turned to women themselves for the pieces of the puzzle that medical science is not prepared to put into place.

Do we all have a diminished interest in sex, or is interest heightened for some of us? Do we all mind the change in our sex lives, if there is one? How do our partners perceive the changes in us? Are they supportive and understanding, or are they hostile and uncommunicative? What do we value most in a relationship at midlife? What least? What changes bother us?

The early questionnaire results indicated that 80 percent of the women experienced hot flashes and night sweats, and between 90 and 95 percent of them were not surprised by them. However, anxiety and irritability (reported by almost as many women as hot flashes) were unexpected by 25 percent. Vaginal dryness, bladder control problems, sleeping difficulties, and mood swings bothered between 50 and 60 percent of the women and were unexpected by 25 to 40 percent of the women. Headaches, experienced by 30 percent of the respondents, were unexpected by almost all of them. The biggest surprise was a marked lack of interest in sex, noted by 30 percent of the women, for which *none* of the women was prepared!

In the chapters that follow, we will delve into the questions and answers and the results of these and other national surveys. At the end of each chapter you will find some thought-provoking questions that you may wish to ask yourself. But first let's examine the stories of four women who agreed to be interviewed in depth about their sex lives at midlife.

We are going to meet a couple, married more than forty years, who reveal how they handled the changes that occurred in their sexual activity, but not in their deep sense of intimacy or in their static state of profound love.

Next, we are going to meet a famous long-widowed vocal artist who is in her seventies and learn of her passionate affair with a married man several years her senior. We will follow them and feel their rediscovered and reignited passion.

A widowed woman in her early sixties describes finding herself single and independent after thirty-five years of happy marriage. Perhaps her elation about her newfound freedom will surprise you.

A lesbian couple and the former lover of one of them disclose the physical and psychological changes that occurred during the perimenopause and after menopause, how those changes affected their sexual relationships, and how they coped with the decade of difference in their ages as they traversed this significant and natural transition in a woman's life.

Forty Years of Marriage—Sex First, Then Love and Intimacy

Sallie looked in the mirror, sucked in her gut, and then gently lifted her walnut-size jowls from her jawbone by pulling the skin of her face upward and toward her ears. She had been going through this same ritual at the mirror for a number of years, wistfully remembering the tautness of her face and the flatness of her abdomen in her younger years. Not too bad for a gal of sixty, she said to herself.

Her husband, Don, went through a similar, though quicker and less obvious ritual each morning when he shaved. The buzzing of the electric razor sounded the same as it had when his cheeks had been pink and full and taut, but he wasn't quite the same, and as he shaved he pulled up his slackened jaw a little to create a smoother surface. Some of the sand in his body had shifted to the bottom of his hourglass just as had Sallie's. Sometimes, he'd look in the mirror and flex his biceps, feeling pleased that they still puffed up. "Not too bad for a man of sixty-one," he would murmur.

Sallie and Don had met in high school in an economics class. It was one of the few courses that Don really enjoyed. It was one of the few classes Sallie detested. Their relationship began when he tried to explain the stock market and the balance of trade to her. Both the relationship and the explanation continued throughout their lives.

The chemistry that drew them together was the glue that kept them together all these years, but the ingredients had changed over the years. In high school, they couldn't wait to get their hands and mouths upon each other. In college, they couldn't wait to hop into bed together. There was this powerful sexual magnet that pulled them toward each other. The couple of years

Don served in the navy made their sexual response to each other even stronger.

After Don was discharged, they got married and over the years had four children. After their first son was born, they subtly shifted from being a couple to being a family. Neither Sallie nor Don can quite remember when their sexual fire began to fizzle. They claim that they were too busy to notice at first. Or, as Sallie explained, "When we finally sat down in the living room at ten P.M. after Don had coached the Little League game and I had driven the ballet class car pool, and the kids were all in their rooms, we crashed. We were happy to sit there and read the morning paper or watch television and wait for the eleven o'clock news. Together."

"Maybe that's when the love attachment becomes just as strong or stronger than the sex drive," said Don, trying to help me understand how sex, love, and intimacy grew and then blended for them.

At some time during that time, the sexual pull relaxed. They still enjoyed sex, but not as often. "That's what made our vacations so special. When we had free time for ourselves, we were like kids again. Couldn't wait to jump into bed. Sometimes, we didn't make it," Sallie added. "I remember the time in Hawaii when we took advantage of an isolated beach cove on Maui," Sallie said as she laughed and blushed.

As the years raced by, love of the family and love of each other were indistinguishable, they both claimed. There were measles, chicken pox, recitals, driving lessons, sports, broken bones, fender benders, graduations, weddings, and the birth of a first grandchild to keep them busy. Don described sex during those years as good, sometimes even great, but not nearly as frequent as they remembered from their early years.

It was shortly after Michael, their first grandchild, was born, that they both remember something going wrong sexually. There was the first time that Don tried to enter Sallie, and the pain was unbearable. The usual amount of foreplay had not produced vaginal lubrication. Then there was the first time Don couldn't get an erection. He couldn't enter her after a night under the stars on the deck of the cruise ship, a night they both agreed had been made for love and lovemaking. The first few times these "problems" occurred, they shyly passed them off, didn't discuss what went wrong, and after a few vain attempts to complete their lovemaking, turned over and went to sleep—or tried to sleep.

Sallie finally got up the guts to raise the issue of the problems with their lovemaking and Don quickly blamed it on job-related stress. Sallie broached the subject again. Don was adamant. Nothing was wrong, he said. "Yes, I love you. No, I'm not having an affair. Nothing is wrong with us. Well, maybe I'm a little preoccupied with some things at the office," he finally admitted.

Sallie and Don, the great communicators, were trying to have sex with an elephant lying between them in bed. Sallie tried to figure out her problem first. She made an appointment for a complete physical and prayed that her internist would ask her about her sex life. He didn't. She tried to get the conversation around to that subject. She couldn't. Finally she mentioned some quirky changes in her menstrual cycle and he suggested that she see her gynecologist. Everything else was "in order," he said.

Next stop, gynecology. She made her annual appointment a few months early and the luckiest event occurred just before she was scheduled. She turned on a television talk show and there we were on *Donahue* discussing great sex after fifty and my then new book, *150 Most-Asked Questions About Menopause: What Women Really Want to Know.* Sallie stopped to listen and couldn't believe her ears. There could be some changes in vaginal lubrication caused by running out of the female hormone estrogen. Now she went to see her gynecologist feeling empowered.

Instead of waiting to see whether he would discuss her symptoms, she began. "Doctor, I think I might be premenopausal. I have some unusual periods of perspiration during the day, and others that wake me soaking wet—even to my hair—at night. My periods have gotten closer together, but now they're further apart, but the flow is much heavier *and,*" she drew in her breath and then burst out, "I get so dry vaginally that I can't enjoy sex. Is this menopause?" she practically whispered.

With a simple blood test that measured the amount of follicle-stimulating hormone (FSH) in her bloodstream, her doctor confirmed that her high FSH levels did indeed indicate she was menopausal. He explained that this finding could account for her hot flashes, her night sweats, and the vaginal thinning and drying that was causing her to experience painful intercourse.

Sallie took her prescription to the drugstore for hormone replacement therapy. She used the 0.5-milligram estrogen patch, changing it twice each week, adding 5 milligrams of progestin each day for the first fourteen days of each month. She also bought a vaginal moisturizer that she had seen advertised. The estrogen and the moisturizer added the vaginal lubrication that she was missing, and Sallie felt up to par sexually.

Don was still having some problems with erections. Sallie insisted that he have a complete physical examination. Nothing wrong there. Of course, Don did not mention his temperamental erection to his internist. So Sallie bought several books about sex and aging and learned how she might be able to help Don get an erection when one eluded him. Their sex life improved after a period of trial and error and with the acknowledgment that they could help each other enjoy sex forever. When they realized that their difficulties were not unusual, but were just the normal changes that can occur as the result of aging, they could communicate about the changes and tell each other what worked best for each of them.

When Sallie and Don agreed to discuss this situation with me they explained they were doing it because they are convinced that more information about midlife sexuality needs to be disseminated, so that couples don't waste their time pretending that nothing is the matter, not talking about it, and even hurting themselves and each other. They both still marvel at the fact that they had to learn from a television talk show, consumer advertisements, and consumer books what was wrong so that they could tell their doctors and get help.

The Song of Sexuality After the Years of Silence

A friend I meet in New York City intermittently for coffee, cocktails, or just good straightforward conversation began one afternoon to share with me the reason for her recent volatility. She is a successful vocalist who had just crossed what she had taken to calling the invisible line of demarcation between ages sixty-nine and seventy, a line that she often described as the separation between middle and old age. I'll call her Jessica.

During our times together Jessica had often rhapsodized about the newfound freedom of her single life, which she had begun to appreciate approximately seven years *after* her husband's death. Once she got used to being alone, she explained, she was no longer lonely. Although she says she loved him dearly, the gnawing sense of missing her husband had ameliorated, and she readily admitted that she was glad to be free of his domineering and driving qualities, which had had a profound and stifling effect on their sexual relationship.

Jessica once told me proudly, "I would not have been an artist without his pushing and his prodding me, but our relationship never ever comforted my soul." So having accepted and found joy in her new status, Jessica, who was then in her mid-sixties, moved into a stunning new art deco apartment that she had designed specifically to reflect her taste and her style, and to address her needs. It was a place, she said, in which she could express her newly discovered, hardwon independence.

She found new self-motivation. She increased her performance schedule, began touring again, took on new teaching commitments, and discovered that she liked having women friends. She liked going to dinner, to concerts, and to the theater with women and she enjoyed traveling with them. Jessica dated occasionally, but each foray into the realm of male-female relationship inevitably reminded her that she would never, could never, give up her rich independent life.

Jessica considered sexual expression to be something she had outgrown and instead spent her passion on her work, her family, and her friends. How could she have known that *he* would reenter her life?

Jessica was just approaching her seventieth birthday—a fact that you'd never have suspected when you looked at her. Attractive and active, her physical appearance and her tremendous enthusiasm belied her years. So it was that one snowy winter night she attended a concert at Lincoln Center and there he was. They had not seen each other for more than thirty years. He was in New York to attend a meeting, he explained. His wife, the third woman to hold that title, had chosen to remain in Palm Springs. Why leave the warm desert for the gales of New York in January?

They began a conversation in the lobby during the first intermission. By the second intermission, they had agreed to have a drink after the performance to catch up on each others' lives. Jessica never heard the rest of the concert. She was shocked by the excitement she felt at this chance meeting. She had relegated these romantic stirrings to the past.

They went out for a nightcap. There was electricity

in the conversation. Surprisingly, there was no strain, no unfamiliarity. She found herself being intense, girlish, and entertaining in turn. He was captivated by her.

It got late and, impulsively, she invited him to see the apartment of which she is so proud. They jumped into a cab and were quickly on the Upper West Side.

He admired everything about the apartment, commenting enthusiastically about its high-tech design. His lavish expressiveness and expansiveness equaled her own. It was almost three o'clock in the morning. Jessica couldn't remember when she had last been up that late. She wasn't tired. There were no yawns that needed to be stifled.

They decided at last to part. She offered to call a cab for him. She lifted the receiver from its cradle slowly, deliberately. It was then that he softly uttered the four words that would change her life. "Don't call the cab," he said.

The ardor of their passion that night was unlike any feelings she had ever known. She revealed to me later that month that until that night, she had believed any spark of sexual desire had been extinguished within her. In fact, Jessica and some of her close friends who admitted that their sexual fires had also turned to cold ashes attributed the loss to the normal aging process. That stormy night in New York, she learned that her sexual giant was merely asleep.

We talk about this often. Jessica has a need to talk about it often. Recently, she shared a piece she read somewhere that she says explains her need to discuss and describe her new lover and her sexual experiences. "Passion makes maniacs and poets. The maniacs want to prolong and refine the rapture, and the poets have to communicate what they've been through. For them passion becomes the only measure of life, the only compensation for dailyness, triviality, and death." Jessica aligns herself with the poets.

So she recalls with me the gymnastic ardor of their first night together, the intensity surpassing anything she has ever experienced. Jessica said candidly, "Everything worked well for each of us. Can it be that our aging bodies are capable still of the intense passion of youth?" This is how it is for Jessica and her lover.

The next months involved plans to meet and inter-mittent phone calls—of which, because he is married, he was in full charge. Jessica suffered. She could not call him. She had to wait and wait. She fully expected each day to come to the realization that it was over. Then he would call. An extravagant gift would arrive. A meeting would be arranged, always subject to the whims of his wife. If at the last minute his wife de-cided to accompany him or not to accompany him, Jessica fit what she now considers the most important part of her life into whatever plan the wife devised. Her life became unbridled chaos.

Jessica threw herself more deeply into her work. She exercised feverishly and ate little. She lost ten pounds and the trimness suited and pleased her. She looked terrific, but she suffered.

At one point he disappeared for a while after telling her that he found the affair too intense, too complicating. Jessica's suffering turned into devastation. "Was this last big chance at happiness going to be wasted? We're both in our seventies: Why should we not grab this happiness, this ecstasy?" Then he called. He could stay away no longer. They had another rapture-filled weekend together and they talked.

Jessica told me that she explained to him that she didn't need to marry him, she didn't need to live with him (although she thought it would be fun), and she didn't need status. All she needed and all she wanted was his love! Their relationship continues to this day, filled with all the passion and pain of youthful love. Is the pleasure wrought of the pain? Their sex life, she tells me, is so complete, so much more satisfying than either one of them has ever experienced before. Yet Jessica is sad. She dares not show her sad face to him, but she tells me that she knows that they are both in the final quarter of their lives and she wishes that they could be together more frequently and more easily and not waste a moment of their remaining years by being apart.

At the 1993 International Menopause Society meeting, held in Stockholm, Sweden, one of the presenters said, "The best way to recharge your sexual battery after midlife is to find a younger mate or an exciting new partner."

For Jessica, that turned out to be true.

Alone, But Never Lonely

Dani loved him when he was alive. She loved him still and she missed him in her way. It was her way that surprised the others who were gathered at my home for the midlife sex discussion group meetings that we were holding that summer. Dani was surprised that we were surprised. She attempted to explain the elation she felt at being single and independent after thirty-five years of marriage.

"It's not what you think," she said. "I don't want you to think for a minute that the joy that I feel now in any way minimizes my marriage." She went on to describe that "her way" had been to compartmentalize her life. There had been the young carefree years, then medical school and the career years that had dovetailed into and grown along with the married years and the family years, and now there were the independent years. These were the "me" years, she explained.

"No stage of my life diminishes any other stage," she asserted. "I wouldn't have wanted to live with anyone other than Sam. We shared thirty-five wonderful years. We raised two wonderful kids. We both worked. We traveled. We reveled in our life together and in our kids' accomplishments, and we derived pleasure from each other's professional lives and from our own.

"But when it was over, it was over. Sam went quickly. A heart attack. One minute he was my partner, the next minute, he was gone. I mourned and I cried and I grieved for quite a while.

"Then I picked myself up and went back to school. Got my master's degree in sociology—something I had always wanted to do. Left medicine for good and began my life anew. And what you fail to comprehend is that this is a new life, and that it is all mine!"

Dani was right. We were so accustomed to offering pity and compassion to widows that we failed to applaud and accept Dani's new life choices. Dani was in her late fifties when she made the transition to an independent single life that involved travel and new experiences. She had even gone on a mountain climbing trip and, as she said, secured herself within herself while hammering pitons into rock and securing herself to the mountain with rope.

"I looked up and I looked down and there was this vast expanse of mountains and sky and me and I knew

I was content. No, I was more than content. I knew I was happy. That night at the campfire at the base of the mountain, one of the men in the group—he was about forty—well, he was at least twenty years my junior—looked at me with interest and I blatantly returned his suggestive look. After the others had drifted off, he asked simply, 'My tent or yours?'

"I said, 'My tent. It's larger.' He stooped to enter the tent and announced candidly, 'I'm happily married and I don't plan to marry you.'

" 'I certainly hope not,' I replied. And I meant it." Dani then told us of the next eight days of breathtaking sunsets followed by sex that left her breathless.

"There was no expectation of more. There was no plaintive voice inside me crying for permanence or for commitment of any sort. There was just all this pleasure and passion. It was so special," she exclaimed. "And I knew that I could have this again when I wanted it, without the ties that bind one down, and I knew that this was how I wanted to live this part of my life."

Dani spoke of her joy in making her own decisions, creating her own plans, taking off for wherever she wanted to go without thought of conforming to someone else's wishes, and she spoke at length of the vitality she found in encountering the unexpected and taking advantage of it when she chose.

This in no way changed the quality or value of the

past, she assured us. Dani is still very involved with her children and her grandchildren and with her career. Yet she might take off tomorrow to go scuba diving off the Great Barrier Reef in Australia or to go skiing in Zermatt.

Dani brought a fresh perspective to our group. Rather than making any attempt to recreate the past, her interest lies in seizing the moment and in creating a fascinating future. She is a very chic and interesting woman, one who is sought after at dinner parties for the brilliance of her conversation and for her lack of pretension. She is entertained, she is entertaining, and she entertains frequently, feeling no need for a host to play opposite her.

I have met many other women who, like Dani, have chosen to embrace midlife sex, love, and intimacy in what is for them new ways. They tell me that their sex lives are not proscribed, but rather are cautiously casual. They value "good safe sex with no strings attached," they say. And they love. They are filled with love of life, love of family, and love of friends. And they have found the ability to enjoy new intimacies within that circle. They now have the ability to become closer and more deeply involved with certain individuals, with their communities, with the planet, and with God. They, too, at this midlife time of their lives wouldn't have it any other way.

Woman to Woman

I wasn't so sure that I would be a good interviewer of this lesbian group, underexposed as I was to the concept of woman love. Yet I knew that this book could not be complete without fully researching all the options that women had for midlife sex, love, and intimacy.

So I asked a physician with whom I frequently lecture whether he could set up some interviews for me with midlife lesbian couples. He was more than willing and able to help as I brought myself face to face with my own lack of knowledge.

The first interview took place in the physician's own office—with three women instead of the couple I had been expecting. Kate, Wilma, and Mary were intelligent and sensitive women who had determined that I needed to talk with all three of them in order to have a complete and honest picture of what had occurred in their relationships at midlife.

When I asked their respective roles in this threesome, it was Kate who spoke first, because she was the central figure, linking these women together.

"I am actually a patient in this office," she explained. "I came here after going through a surgical menopause when I was forty-two years old. I had had myriad problems that had begun in my thirties. When my doctor described the purpose of your interview, I asked both Wilma, my current lover, and Mary, my lover at the time that I went through menopause, to come with me, because it was obvious to me that you should talk to them both."

How right she was! These three bright and articulate professional women with their honesty and compassion taught me more that day than any amount of reading and research could have afforded me. Their comfort with each other created my comfort as well. We began to discuss how premenopause and changing hormone levels affected them and other lesbian couples with whom they had discussed this process.

"First of all," Kate said, "let me tell you that I don't think a man would ever have given me the concern, care, or compassion that Mary did throughout our relationship.

"It's been seven years since I had a hysterectomy due to massive fibroid tumors. I had a really rough time. I was thirty-five. My gynecologist was treating surgical menopause with estrogen pills and they weren't doing for me what they were supposed to do. I got very depressed. I was riding a roller coaster—not only by the month, but even on a daily basis. I dutifully took my estrogen pill in the morning right after I brushed my teeth. The pill peaked each day at about two P.M. I was fine until then, but by evening, my estrogen level would drop drastically. I went to bed at night and couldn't sleep. I didn't want anything to do with anybody. Don't touch me. Don't come near me. I would have hot flashes at night, all night. It was horrible. I kicked the dog, the cat, I was mean to Mary's child— our child. I felt depressed, even suicidal. I began seeing a therapist who said, 'Come on—you can handle it!'

"This menopause nightmare was the final stroke in our dying relationship. We hadn't been doing well for a long time, although we really tried.

"No, it wasn't the sex. In the seven years we were together, we had never had sex! I just wasn't interested and that was long before menopause," Kate admitted.

Now Mary spoke for the first time: "And no sexual expression was making me crazy." Mary had been married and had had a son. She'd left her abusive husband years earlier even before she realized that she was a homosexual. She had met Kate while both were working at a career camp. They had been together several summers before she realized that she loved her.

Kate explained that she fell head over heels for Mary that first summer, but knew that Mary had been a married woman—"obviously heterosexual, I thought"—and so she chose just to accept and be satisfied with the sociability of a caring coworker. One summer, something changed. Mary seemed more vulnerable. She began to describe the overwhelming problems she had had to overcome. She spoke of a husband who drank and who beat her when he was drunk. The admission of this troubled past gave Kate the courage to approach Mary in a new way. Slowly, tenderly they became lovers—lovers with no sex.

Mary said, "As a couple, we tried real hard to please each other. I wanted sex, she didn't, but we loved each other and we both wanted to stay together."

"Now with Wilma," Kate interjected, speaking about her current lover, "who went through the change after me, I, too, think I was more sensitive and understanding of her menopause transition and changing hormones than a male mate would be.

"It was so different in this relationship. When Wilma first experienced some changes, her doctor met with both of us. He took me into the examination room with her. He treated us like a couple. He didn't say, 'It's all in your head—grow up.' Instead, he checked her hormone levels. We got through this as a lesbian couple because we were able to go through it together. Men don't understand menopause the way we do. We could be totally supportive to each other. We understood. Imagine that with a man!"

Before they came to meet with me, the three women had had lunch together and discussed the sexual connection that had been missing between Kate and Mary. Kate said it was probably because of the "abusive stuff" in her past. "I masturbated as a child as an attention-grabber, always making sure that my mother caught me. She beat me for it every time.

"Nothing turned me on," Kate continued. "So Mary and I saw a sex therapist, spent lots of money. Nothing helped, but we loved each other enough to be together without sex. We had hugging, kissing, caressing, and true loving. I didn't know then that I could have offered to bring Mary to orgasm, or I would have. She never asked, because she knew I wasn't into the sex thing.

"After I saw this gynecologist, I had my first shot of testosterone. When it kicked in, Mary and I planned a trip to the Carribean islands. That was as close as we ever got to having sex; that was as amorous as I ever got with Mary. But sex just didn't happen for us. It was probably too late in our relationship.

"I've been using testosterone pellet implants ever since and they sparked a searing fire in me with the woman I saw after Mary and I split up. My new lover and I had good sex and I've had good sex ever since. Wilma and I now enjoy a normal sex life. The androgen therapy saved my life. I had probably been testosterone deficient since puberty. I had always been fatigued. I never had any energy—let alone sexual energy."

Now Mary picked up the story. "Even after she was on testosterone, Kate's lack of information about what she felt and what to do with her feelings hung on. I would lie naked next to her in bed, but I could not force her into a sexual loving state.

"Why didn't I leave sooner? I'm seven years older than Kate, you know. I had had only one other relationship with a woman when I was in college, but she was so conservative that she would only have sex with me on the weekends and would go with a guy during the week. She convinced me that what we were doing was wrong. So in grad school I got married and we adopted a son. I stayed married to an abusive, mentally ill man for five years. After I left him, I dated men, but I had crushes on women. I continued to push those feelings down. Then that summer, I met Kate and I was happy. I knew then that I was a lesbian. I didn't leave Kate because I loved her and I didn't know what else was out there for me."

Today Mary is in a happy, sexually fulfilling relationship with Penny and she and Kate are still good friends. They are both convinced that going through these problems as women together made everything easier.

Kate's new love, Wilma, had been married for fifteen years. The love and intimacy that Kate found with Wilma had been tightly tied to sex. "In my relationship with Wilma, the sexual end was real important, because I was right in the middle of my new testosterone-stimulated puberty. At first we had sex constantly, trying all sorts of new things. We've been together for five years and have lived together for the last four years. Our sex life has slowed down now. Wilma works nights and has chosen to have the kids remain with their dad, but we have Wilma's kids every other weekend."

"Do the kids know that you are lesbians?" I asked.

Wilma remarked that she had researched for some time to find the best time to tell kids, which she explained is before puberty. When they were very young, she had taken them to the dentist's office, which just happened to be upstairs from an abortion clinic where picketers were rallying.

"It was an ideal opening for me," Wilma recalled. "We looked out of the dentist's office windows and started talking about how differences set off controversy: 'See the placards; see the anger? That's because people see things differently, and sometimes one group tries to regulate or stifle the other.'

"When the time seemed right to tell my children, I recalled for them the scene we had witnessed in front of the abortion clinic. Then I explained my lesbianism and told them that my lifestyle could also be considered controversial and although I had no problem with their telling about it, I wanted them to be careful whom they told. It went well.

"I think our physician is unique. My experience here was unique. I was desperate to understand completely who I was. Kate suggested that I talk to her doctor. I don't talk to men much; my community of friends is made up of women. He helped me see my way to the real me. I don't think I have ever gotten the kind of empathy I needed from any other man—sympathy, yes, but not empathy. Sometimes men want to be patted on the back. I remember when I was still married and my husband would say proudly, expectantly waiting for groveling appreciation, "I babysat the kids." I always wanted to ask him, "Just whose kids did you take care of?"

Mary, the oldest of the women, helped sum it up. "In a lesbian relationship there is usually equal responsibility, and this is also an intimacy issue. For example, I make more money than my mate, Penny. She has more skills in the home. There was a moment when I caught myself thinking that she needed to do more at home since she had the skills and contributed less money. But I caught myself and was conscious that I was pulling that male thing, so we negotiated instead. In my experience, men can't get intimate enough to say let's negotiate. Maybe it's because men and women are filled with the stereotypes even when we think we're not. With another woman, you can be 'at one.' You can communicate differently—better—on all levels, about philosophy, religion, sex, and childrearing and this good-quality communication enables us to resolve issues differently than we can with men. The superior level of communication expands to include the organizations we choose to be part of and to the friends we choose to make. This is real intimacy, and it incorporates and involves all of who you are. We do it differently—it is because we are more alike, not only in our body design, but in our rearing and how we grew up, in what was expected of us, in who we are, and in how we tick.

"Sex, love, and intimacy in a lesbian relationship follow no preset roles. With us, everything is up for grabs, from whether we have orgasms together or separately. Do we use our vibrators at the same time or, if not, who goes first? Are we interested in vaginal or clitoral orgasm?

"Lesbian relationships are bound together with the glue of working things out together. It's a miracle that we can make it work, because of how society views us. We work out our social lives, our personal lives, we work out sex, we work out orgasm, we love our mates, and we think we represent the ultimate in intimacy."

As we concluded the interview, Kate said gently, "I have a right to be who I am and to find love my way. You know, we all do." Of course, we do.

PROPERTY OF
CAPE FEAR MEMORIAL HOSPITAL
LIBRARY

CHAPTER 2

What Is the
Role of Sexuality
at Midlife?

THERE IS A ROLE for our sexuality throughout our lives. In order to understand how to maintain our sexual vitality at midlife, we need to understand where sexuality begins.

The Anatomy of Sex

Even before we are born, there are hormonal actions that shape us, prepare us for puberty, and enable us to reproduce. The primary sex hormones are the female sex hormones, estrogen and progesterone, and the male hormone, testosterone, which is one of the androgen hormones—the hormones that promote masculinization. In both women and men, it is the male hormone, testosterone, that creates our libido, regulating our sexual desire, responsiveness, and performance.

Although androgens are male sex hormones, they are produced in men and women alike and seem to control the libido for both. How, then, does a male hormone govern a woman's sexuality? The answer begins at our birth.

At birth, our ovaries contain approximately 500,000 eggs—all of the eggs we will ever have. These eggs remain intact as we spend our first ten to thirteen years nonreproductively.

Then, at puberty, estrogen production surges. Puberty brings with it our first menstrual cycle. Until menopause (the time after our last menstrual cycle), we usually can reproduce. After menopause (the average age for which is 51.4), we enter our nonreproductive years.

From our first to our last menstrual cycles, a complicated symphony plays between our brain and our ovaries that casts our sex hormones into the following roles. The hypothalamus gland, located at the base of the brain in the center of the skull, sends signals to the pituitary gland, located in the base of the skull. The pituitary gland then produces the follicle-stimulating hormone (FSH) and the luteinizing hormone (LH) that directly affect the growth and development of the ovarian follicle, the sac containing an egg. The FSH stimulates the follicle to ripen and the LH matures the egg and causes its release from the follicle.

The powerful ovaries control the reproductive system. They secrete the female sex hormones estrogen and progesterone to prepare the lining of the uterus for a fertilized egg should a pregnancy occur. If it does not, the estrogen and progesterone are shed in our monthly period and the cycle begins again. All the while, the ovaries are also producing a small amount of testosterone—ten to twenty times less than a man produces in his gonads and adrenal glands.

Normally this cyclic rhythm continues throughout our reproductive years, perhaps interrupted occasionally by pregnancy. Then, when we have run out of our preprogrammed number of eggs and the FSH and LH can no longer stimulate the ovary to produce an egg or the estrogen and progesterone that follow, we enter the menopause.

We may run out of eggs earlier than the average age and then go into premature menopause, generally considered to be before age forty. Surgical menopause may occur at any age when the uterus and the ovaries are removed in a procedure called a hysterectomy, with a bilateral oopherectomy.

In some women, the testosterone that they also produced in their ovaries also lessens or stops at menopause. And although the adrenal glands, which also produce testosterone, may continue to do so, the testosterone in our systems may be reduced by 50 percent or more. We know that it is testosterone that creates our libido, so during the perimenopause or after menopause, we may lose interest in sex if our testosterone production dips significantly. Conversely, if we do not lose testosterone and it is no longer opposed by the other female sex hormones, we may have an increased interest in sex. Each woman's menopause is unique!

The adrenal glands in both men and women produce androgens in approximately equal amounts. The androgens then travel via the bloodstream to the liver, where they are converted into testosterone. For many women, the small amount of testosterone that they end up with after menopause may be enough to keep their libido intact. Others may end up feeling sexually unresponsive—even sexually dead.

It should also be noted that there are many factors other than testosterone that enter into our sexual responsiveness. We have to consider the degree of attraction we feel for our partner, the excitement that the sexual encounter holds for us, how much stress we are under, our partner's state of mind and state of health, and what else is going on in our lives that distracts us from being interested in our sexuality.

We have learned from the interviews with Sallie and Don, Jessica, Dani, and Kate, Mary, and Wilma just how different the impact of sexuality at midlife can be. Part of the problem in understanding sexuality rests in our puritanical backgrounds. "Sexy seniors," someone once said to me, "are a contradiction in terms." No way!

The need for sexual expression need not diminish as we age, although some women at midlife state that they feel that their desires are "unseemly." Let's look at the concept of midlife. The midlife transition for men used to be considered to be ages forty to forty-five, according to the late Yale Professor Daniel J. Levinson, principal author of *The Seasons of a Man's Life.* This period was followed by the middle adult era, which extended to age sixty and into the late adult era. Levinson's seminal work separated a man's life into stages or eras. Although women were not included in his study, recent research indicates that women also appear to go through specific developmental periods. In *Passages,* author Gail Sheehy's research, and thus the book, culminated with women's passage into their fifties.

Today, however, given our longer lifespans, the transition periods have changed for both men and women. A man who is healthy today at fifty will probably live beyond his early seventies; a woman healthy at fifty may live well into her mid-eighties or longer. These extended lifespans have greatly expanded the midlife transition for both men and women.

The leading edge of the baby boomers no longer accepts forty as the onset of midlife; rather, midlife is now informally considered to be a prolonged period beginning somewhere in the forties and extending well into the sixties, even into our seventies. I consider midlife to extend to as late in life as we remain healthy. Why, then, is a discussion of midlife sex deemed unseemly?

In seminar after seminar and lecture after lecture from New England to Southern California, I continue to observe an unwillingness to bring midlife sexual issues onto the main stage. Sexual issues are eagerly discussed in the small-group gatherings that occur after the formal program and after the open question-and-answer period. They are the subjects of the questions and comments that are sent to me anonymously on the backs of my sex, love, and intimacy questionnaires. Is it any wonder that curiosity and concern are unsatisfied when we consider that the most recent publication about menopause from the National Institutes of Health, National Institute of Aging (December 1992), provides just a few paragraphs under the subheading "What About Sex?" and that "The Harvard Health Letter Special Report," "Postmenopausal Hormone-Replacement Therapy" (October 1993) contains only one paragraph devoted to sexual difficulties?

June M. Reinisch, director emerita of the Kinsey Institute for Research in Sex, Gender, and Reproduction, explains it this way: "Our country is still very uptight about sex. It's still a taboo subject. People born between 1910 and 1935 are very conservative sexually." They are conservative because they were brought up in an era when good sex education wasn't available. At least sex is now discussed openly on television, radio, and in magazines, newspapers, and books.

Regardless of your age or stage of life, you are going to find direct and useful answers to your questions about sex, love, and intimacy in this book. Although the sex survey results show that most of the questionnaires—almost 80 percent—were returned by married women, one wonders whether that indicates that most of the attendees at the meetings were married, or whether more married women chose to complete the questionnaire. Looking at the results of the larger study (15,000 questionnaires), it is apparent that the audiences were fairly evenly divided between married and single women, so it seems obvious that greater numbers of married women chose to respond to the sex survey, possibly because they had a partner.

To gain a perspective on midlife sex, it is important to know the age breakdown of the respondents to my sex questionnaire. A full 79 percent were between the ages of forty and fifty-four, with the greatest number of these (49 percent) between the ages of forty-five and forty-nine. Ten percent of the questionnaires came from women between fifty-five and fifty-nine years of age; 4½ percent came from women ages thirty-five to forty, and another 4 percent from women ages sixty to sixty-four. The remaining 2½ percent were completed by women ages sixty-five to seventy-four. These age ranges are similar to those on the 15,000 questionnaires I utilized in my first two books in this series, but the numbers have changed and now include more younger women.

In response to the first item on the survey: "In my middle years my interest in sex has____not changed____heightened____diminished____disappeared," 48 percent of the respondents indicated that their interest in sex had diminished or disappeared. Responding to item two, "I find this change to be____satisfactory____exciting____disturbing, or____a relief, most respondents indicated that they found this change to be disturbing. Of the 22 percent who indicated that their interest in sex had heightened, most women found the change exciting. (Unmarried women were two to three times more likely to say that their interest in sex had heightened, and most of them considered this change exciting.) The 30 percent that stated that their sex drive was unchanged indicated that they found this "satisfactory." Three percent found the change to be a relief.

From this sampling we also learned that almost half of the respondents wanted to recharge their sexual batteries. So is trying to understand and improve our sex lives at midlife "unseemly"? Absolutely not!

Obviously, hormonal changes that occur with menopause have to be taken into consideration when we discuss midlife sex and we'll cover those changes in Chapter 3. But there are numerous other changes that occur in our lives that impact our sex lives as well. Obviously, the loss of a partner is the number-one factor, and we'll answer questions about finding partners in Chapter 9 and questions about solo sex in Chapter 12. For now, let's broaden our perspective about events that can change our sex lives by considering a letter that was written to me on the back of a questionnaire after a seminar in the Northwest:

I have always been interested in sex and have enjoyed all aspects of it within a loving relationship with my husband. Although my interest has diminished somewhat, what with age and hormones and all, I have not lost my desire or the feelings associated with sex at all.

My problem is that my husband won't have sexual intercourse at all since becoming a displaced executive two and a half years ago. He is affectionate with hugs, kisses, kindness, and even an occasional foot massage, but that's it these days. Short of the act itself and some intimate touching, that's all I can expect from him.

He won't discuss this with me. I have spoken to my doctor about it, but he can't offer any concrete help. He says I'm doing the right thing. What's that mean?

My marriage is thirty-seven years old, my life is filled with children and grandchildren and there is not another woman to contend with either. This is so perplexing and I see no way out since my husband acknowledges no problem.

I take care of myself, look good for my age, and have a full life. What's missing? A little sexual intercourse in my life. I'm not asking for much, am I? You have to say NO!

The sexual turnoff here appears to have come from an event that occurred outside the relationship which resulted in a significant change in the man's life, both in his work life and in his sense of self-esteem and self-worth. These are the kinds of change-of-life issues that have not received enough attention. My writer is fifty-seven years old and she's deeply disappointed and suffering. Her mate is probably suffering, too. This is a good example of the type of situation for which this book will be especially helpful, enabling a couple to use the information contained herein as a springboard to good honest communication and helping them to work through the problem or giving them the incentive and courage to address the problem with the help of a counselor or a therapist.

In an interview with me, psychiatrist Stephen B. Levine, M.D., co-director of the Center for Marital and Sexual Health in Cleveland, Ohio, and clinical professor of psychiatry at Case Western Reserve University School of Medicine, described the initial difficulties that people have to sort through before they make that first appointment. "To get help for a psychological matter, we have to overcome our narcissism. That's part of the American tradition of self-sufficiency. If I come for help, it's an acknowledgment that I can't solve the problem myself and it's part of our Puritan heritage to be self-sufficient." We have to rise above that and get help!

What becomes clear is that the role of sexuality in midlife, like the midlife transition itself, does not have a clear, concise definition or definite lines of demarcation. It is all individual: the product of who we are, what we want, how we see ourselves, and what we are willing to do to achieve our goals.

Yet most of us are interested in norms, particularly those relating to sexual frequency. The questions and answers that follow will offer what some of the experts consider to be the norms and will provide the averages, but as you consider the answers it is important that you remain aware that an average is only an average taken from the mean, and that there are broad deviations to the mean, particularly when it comes to your sex life. What is good and right for you *is* what is good and right for you.

Years ago, famed researcher Helen S. Kaplan, M.D., Ph.D., director of the human sexuality program at Cornell Medical Center, identified the ages when sexual desire peaks in women and in men. From her work, we learned that females peak at thirty-eight years of age and men at seventeen. Perhaps this accounts for the fact that throughout life men and women may be strange bedfellows. Yet Dr. Kaplan also taught us that one of the last functions to decline with age is our sexual function! That means that women and men can enjoy sexually fulfilling lives into their nineties and even later. This book will provide guidelines to help you to keep your sexual flame burning as brightly as the candles that you are collecting in ever-increasing numbers on your birthday cake.

We need to understand what sparks our sexual libido and how it works in order to learn how we can enhance, regain, or restart our sexual selves. So let's look at the anatomy of sexual response:

1. I consider myself sexy. How important is sex at midlife?

It depends on how you define sex and it depends on you. If you define having sex solely as engaging in sexual intercourse, it may be more or less important depending on your interest, your physical ability, your partner's physical and psychological availability, and the pleasure and satisfaction you derive from the act. If, however, you expand your definition of sex to include the whole realm of lovemaking—from initial attraction and flirting to touching, caressing, massaging, licking, sucking, and all of the fantasies and feelings that go with these acts—you are talking about human contact that is normally vital to everyone.

The unavailability of a partner and the concern about safer sex or the choice of going it alone do not make sex at midlife less important, either. If you enjoy the feelings that accompany being sexually turned on, if you find orgasm a tension reducer or a sleep enhancer, there is no reason to give up one of life's greatest pleasures. In Chapter 12, there are important questions and useful answers about self-stimulation and masturbation.

2. How often do most women at midlife want to engage in sexual intercourse?

There is no norm with which I can answer that question. Going back to our questionnaires, we can see that women whose interest in sex is diminished or has disappeared are disappointed (48 percent) and disturbed by that fact. Fully 93 percent indicated that they wanted to learn ways to increase their interest in sex and more than 90 percent were interested in ways to stimulate their sexual satisfaction.

The women whose interest in sex is unchanged find

that satisfactory, yet a full 40 percent of those respondents would still like to increase their interest in sex and their sexual satisfaction. Further, as noted, those who have experienced heightened interest in sex are excited about it. One fifty-seven-year-old single woman actually indicated on her questionnaire that in her middle years her interest in sex had heightened and she found that to be a relief, adding this gratuitous note of explanation, "It is a relief that I can finally outdo men!"

3. What is the average number of times a week that couples at midlife and older have sex?

Many experts indicate that midlife couples on average have sex fewer than two times a week. It appears from the survey that a great number of the women would like to engage in sex more frequently. *The Janus Report on Sexual Behavior,* authored by Samuel S. Janus, Ph.D., and Cynthia L. Janus, M.D., states that 58 percent of women and 46 percent of men considered themselves to be functioning below their maximum sexual potential. According to Estelle Ramey, M.D., Ph.D., professor emeritus and senior physiologist at Georgetown University School of Medicine, "Intercourse tends to slacken off in terms of the number of times per week, particularly in long-term relationships, although that does not mean that the enjoyment is not there." On the question of frequency, Dr. Reinisch comments, "The answer to that is that there is no answer. One of the factors that has to do with frequency is the newness of the relationship. It's not the only factor. . . . There are couples who have sex three times a day for their entire marriage. . . . If it's once a day, once a month, or once a year, if both members of the couple are happy, it's the right frequency for them."

The newest survey, published in *The Social Organization of Sexuality* and co-authored by University of Chicago sociologists Edward Laumann, Stuart Michaels, and Robert Michael, tells us that in terms of frequency, Americans fall into three groups. One third have sex twice a week or more, one third just a few times a month, and the last one third have sex a few times a year or not at all.

The simplest and most direct answer comes from Alex Comfort, M.D. In his book *The New Joy of Sex,* he notes that "the right frequency for sex is as often as you and your partner enjoy it." Ellen Rosenblatt, M.D., director of the Program for Women at the Center for Marital and Sexual Health and assistant clinical professor of psychiatry at Case Western Reserve University School of Medicine, thinks that the question goes deeper and would ask, "Why are individuals asking about frequency? If I say to you that normal is twice a week or three times a week, what would you do with that information?" Psychologist Stanley Althof, co-director of the Center for Marital and Sexual Health and associate professor of psychology in Urology at Case Western Reserve University, adds that the subject of frequency "has to be taken in context. What else is going on in the couple's lives . . . do they have two little kids and are they both working and tired all the time? What is the context of the couple's life?" Obviously, myriad factors must be considered when an answer to the question of the frequency of sexual intercourse is considered.

4. Does sexual function decline with age?

Compared to when we were eighteen, chances are that at midlife and even later, the complexities of life enter into our sexual functioning, and although sex is important throughout life, its expression changes. As we age, hormones play vital roles in the process and may shape our sexual changes, particularly for women. Typically men have fewer and less dramatic hormonal changes than women. Although their testosterone levels do not drop precipitously, they may produce less testosterone as the years pass, and other gradual changes may include less response to the testosterone. Basically, however, most men who do not incur serious illness or disease will continue to produce testosterone, sperm, and semen as long as they live. But men have their own problems and women and men should be aware that mens' sexual function does decline somewhat after the age of fifty. Men may require additional stimulation in order to gain an erection and may need longer rest periods between erections.

Women undergo much more dramatic changes at midlife. In my book *150 Most-Asked Questions About Menopause,* I describe the changes that occur as women's lowering levels of sex hormones change their menstrual cycle. This may begin to affect their sexual function as many as ten to fifteen years prior to menopause. The loss of hormones at menopause then can have a dramatic effect, sometimes causing painful intercourse or a lack of interest in sex. Sexuality and menopause are discussed in Chapter 3.

It is true that physical changes are associated with aging, and that sexual function may decline somewhat along with those changes. However, there are many avenues we can pursue to counter those changes and to work to keep desire strong, including exercise, proper diet, stress reduction, quitting smoking, not abusing alcohol or drugs, regular physical examinations, a positive attitude, good self-esteem, a comfortable body image, and taking hormones or pursuing alternative therapies if they are appropriate for us. Dr. Ramey says that it is "nonsense to think that sexuality becomes irrelevant even into old age."

5. *Is oral sex more common among older adults?*

The Janus Report indicated that more than 88 percent of men and 87 percent of women perform oral sex (cunnilingus and fellatio) on a regular basis and that it has become an acceptable means of achieving orgasm for them. Other earlier studies indicate that 50 to 80 percent of women perform fellatio. A study of Americans reported in *The Kinsey Institute New Report on Sex* by June M. Reinisch, Ph.D., also indicates that oral sex is common among older couples. This study shows that 56 percent of the men gave oral sex and 49 percent of women reported receiving it. The enjoyment factor is even higher: 82 percent of the women and 95 percent of the men reported enjoying oral sex. The new Chicago study, not surprisingly, tells us that when it comes to oral sex, both men and women think it is better to receive than to give.

To stimulate your male partner so that he can achieve an erection and sustain it long enough for him to ejaculate, try a slow steady hand massage, beginning in the genital area and moving to the penis. This may or may not be followed by oral sex. Dr. June Reinisch suggests that if you have not given oral sex before, you may begin slowly to get used to the idea of taking the penis in your mouth by first stroking the genital area, then the penis, then giving small kisses, and that you do this over time—by this she means weeks or months—so that when oral sex is arrived at you are comfortable with it. For safest sex, some experts recommend that you suck on the condom-sheathed penis only until ejaculation is imminent and that you remove your mouth at that time. If no condom is used, remove your mouth when ejaculation is imminent and permit your partner to ejaculate in his hand or on his abdomen or on an area of your body where there is no cut or skin abrasion.

6. *Does sexual activity remain constant in older women?*

It can, and as our survey shows, it does for many women. Many other women wish it did. There are many factors that can interrupt sexual activity as we age. Our libido can be changed by many internal and external forces. A change in our health or the health of our mate can dramatically lessen our interest and our abilities. Other factors prevail as well. Certain illnesses such as high blood pressure and diabetes and the medications used in their treatment can render men virtually impotent. Drugs to fight anxiety and depression can also deaden desire. For example, one of the side effects of Valium and other so-called minor tranquilizers and anti-anxiety drugs may be a diminution in our sex drive. This can be true of many other diseases and physical disabilities and the medications used to treat them as well. These are side effects that you will want to discuss with your partner and your physician.

This question leads us right into the "use it or lose it" edict for remaining sexually active and satisfied. For example, the occurrence of vaginal atrophy is significantly lower in sexually active women because of the increased lubrication that is stimulated by arousal and rubbing and the good muscle tone that occurs from using those muscles. Today, estrogen in its many forms— from vaginal cream to pill, patch, and injection—is used to ward off vaginal thinning and drying. There are also a number of very good vaginal moisturizers on the market that are available over the counter that women report help them enormously. (More about moisturizers in Chapter 3.)

The "use it or lose it" adage applies to women in terms of both vaginal lubrication and orgasmic response, which would lead us to assume that sexual activity could remain constant in older women if they remained sexually active.

In terms of sexual activity and long-term relationships another question you would have to have the answer to and, obviously, you can't, is: If he had a new partner, would he become erect more easily, and if she had a new partner, would she secrete enough lubrication naturally to make sex comfortable?

7. I don't mind not having a strong sexual drive anymore. Is there anything wrong with me?

As described earlier, sexual drive is comprised of many factors in our lives and is stimulated by testosterone, one of our androgen hormones, as explained in "The Anatomy of Sex" at the beginning of this chapter. As we age there are often lower amounts of those hormones circulating in our bloodstreams to encourage sexual interest. If you are comfortable and happy as you are, be assured there is nothing wrong with you sexually. If you are concerned, check it out with your physician. Occasionally one or another of a couple in a long-term relationship handles sexual dissatisfaction by finding a lover, as the danger, the novelty, and the mystery of the forbidden relationship may make them desire more sex during that period of time.

I have a friend who tells me that she and her husband of many years are quite content hugging, kissing, and holding hands, and that they do not miss the sexual gymnastics of their youth at all. In fact, she says that inasmuch as they believe sex could never be as it was, they don't want to disappoint themselves now or to tarnish the memory of their blazing sex of the past. That's okay, too.

8. *How can I get more aroused from foreplay?*

First of all, you have to determine what arouses you the most. Try to stay with your sexual urges as they occur to learn what kinds of preludes to intercourse or to other routes to orgasm work best for you. For example, is it when your nipples are stroked, kissed, or sucked? Or is it when your clitoris is rubbed? Make sure you communicate to your partner what works best for you and try to indicate how long you need and want that particular form of love play to go on. As we age, and with the loss of estrogen at menopause, our sexuality can be affected in many ways. Since our skin, our largest organ, is replete with estrogen receptors that no longer receive estrogen after menopause, skin sensitivity may be reduced, and our partners need to be aware of that. They need to know that if the same gentle touch that drove you wild isn't working, they may need to increase the pressure or try stroking you in a new place. You've got to experiment. There may also be neural, vibratory, smell, and taste sensations that are affected by estrogen loss. The quality and quantity of vaginal secretions may be reduced and the vaginal tissue may become thinner and dryer, making intercourse uncomfortable or even painful. Many of these problems can be solved by replacing your estrogen. You may want to discuss the various forms of estrogen replacement with your physician. If estrogen is not an option for you, discuss other possibilities with your own doctor. You may also want to experiment to learn what excites you most. Often erotic literature or videos can stimulate arousal, and many couples routinely watch them prior to or even during lovemaking. Give up smoking and excessive amounts of alcohol, which can sabotage arousal and sexuality in both men and women by dulling the senses.

9. *How do I handle sex emotionally when I have the desire, but it seems unimportant to me to make the effort?*

Casey, one of the women in the discussion group, posed a similar question. Mediterranean-looking and slim of waist and thigh, she said that she and her retired husband get up each morning and work out strenuously. In the afternoon they play golf or tennis, and they usually have a date with another couple for dinner, bridge, or a movie. When they return home, they're tired. They get into bed and fall right to sleep. When they do remember to have sex, they both enjoy it and often remark to each other, "That was so nice. We should do it more often." Obviously, they are emotionally fulfilled through their love and their intimate sharing of other activities. If the effort to initiate sex seems too great for you, check to see if you are otherwise content in your relationship. If not, make the effort and you may find even greater fulfillment. Just remember that love and intimacy are expressed in many ways over the years, often in ways that are as fulfilling as when a couple is younger.

10. Should I expect that sexual activity will become less and less frequent, less and less important, and then stop altogether?

I wouldn't expect that at all. I think that if we are healthy and our partners are healthy, we can, as Dr. Kaplan discovered, engage in sexual activity into our nineties and even later. But changes in our lives can alter the availability of that activity, and changes in our extrasexual activities may lessen its importance to us. All in all, we need to begin to view the role of sexuality and sexual activity in midlife and beyond on an individual basis, understanding that there are vast differences in desire at all ages and that there is no right or wrong way to express this aspect of our emotional well-being. Indeed, data from a number of important studies (such as the longitudinal study at the Duke University Center for the Study of Aging and Human

Development) demonstrates that some women's interest in sex accelerates as they grow older. Other studies by Masters and Johnson, Kinsey, the National Institute of Aging, and the National Institute of Mental Health indicate that individuals who were sexually active in their younger years frequently remain sexually active as they age. All kinds of studies on frequency as we age come up with a variety of answers. Dr. Ramey cites one not-too-uncommon extreme: "A woman, for example, who all her life has been anorgasmic almost welcomes the cessation of intercourse or the slackening of it because it never played a central role in a relationship for her anyway." Dr. Levine reminds us that "what people feel, including their sexual desire, has something to do with the multiple contexts in which their lives are embedded." So, for the many of us who are within the ill-defined range of midlife today—somewhere between age forty and illness or infirmity—and whether or not we participated in the sexual revolution, there is no reason for us not to participate in and encourage a midlife and late-life sexual revelation.

"There is no such thing as best in a world of individuals."

—Hugh Prather
Notes to Myself: My struggle to become a person
Bantam Books, 1976

Questions for You

1. Is engaging in sexual activity important to you?

2. Are you satisfied with the role sex plays in your life?

3. Does your frequency of sexual intercourse please you?

4. Do you engage in oral sex?

5. Are you in a long-term relationship?

CHAPTER 3

How Do Hormones
Affect Our
Sexual Selves?

M. E. TED QUIGLEY, M.D., was most helpful to me in the writing of this book, providing not only information, but also patients I could interview to learn the effect of hormones upon our sexual selves. I met Dr. Quigley, a reproductive endocrinologist, in December 1992, at a program at which we both lectured in La Jolla California, having been invited by Sharp Memorial Hospital. With the publication of my books on menopause and osteoporosis, I was invited back to La Jolla by Dr. Quigley and Scripps Health. On a Saturday morning in late October 1993, we presented a program to more than a thousand women. Everyone had the opportunity to participate—physicians, women on the program telling their stories, women from the audience, and me. It was a resounding success!

Through Dr. Quigley, I met Daphne, age forty-five. Daphne, a slim, stunning, cultured blonde, had become Dr. Quigley's patient about four years earlier. She had sought him out because her periods would stop for three months and then return. More important, she was also experiencing not just a lack of interest in sex, but an active distaste for it.

"The sexual aversion thing got worse and I came in to see Dr. Quigley. I was at the point that I didn't want my husband to touch me. I didn't want anything sexual at all. I was just dead!"

Daphne described her husband, Dan, as so supportive that he brought home erotic videotapes to help her and began reading books about menopause so that he could try to understand what she was going through.

"I wouldn't read any of the books at first," Daphne said. "I wouldn't agree that menopause was what this was about. Finally, I gave in. Everything I read about menopause described what was happening to me.

"My original doctor didn't want to help me," Daphne said. "He didn't want to put me on estrogen. He said I was too young. He said I would just have to live this way for a while. So I began asking around about a new doctor and that's how I found Dr. Quigley."

After providing Dr. Quigley with a complete medical history during which she described the classical menopause symptoms—hot flashes, night sweats, insomnia, mood swings, headaches, and others—and a comprehensive physical examination, a simple blood test measuring her follicle-stimulating hormone (FSH) confirmed the fact that Daphne was indeed going through menopause. A serum testosterone test confirmed that her ovaries had also declined their testosterone production. Dr. Quigley prescribed estrogen and cyclic progestin and an injection of testosterone to be given once each month. According to Daphne, during that first month there was a small but noticeable improvement in her sex drive.

"During the second month I just went bonkers. I don't know if I had been given too high a dose of the testosterone or whether I reacted too strongly to it, but I thought I went too far with my sexual activity. I'm still out of character in some of the things that I'm doing. I fantasize a lot and my husband and I are still doing things that are clearly out of character for me."

She asserted, however, that she is comfortable with her accelerated and innovative sexuality and that her husband is very happy with the change in their sex lives, too. Daphne described her whole new sexual persona without embarrassment.

"I now want to wear sexy underwear and risqué outfits. I buy push-up bras with no covering over the top of my breasts. It makes me feel good to push them out. I do it for me as much as for Dan."

Daphne explained that the testosterone shot kicks in in about four or five days and lasts one and a half to two weeks. During the last week of the month she is aware that it is wearing off, but Dr. Quigley permits her to have only one shot per month. A side effect of the testosterone therapy has been the growth of heavy blond hair on her chin, which she has removed with wax every three weeks. The hair growth and an occasional pimple on her face don't bother her. She is concerned sometimes about her increased interest in sex: She feels activities she creates surrounding sex are "sometimes bizarre," but then at the end of the month when the shot wears off, she feels like her "normal self" and finds it comforting to know that she is the same, even though she misses her sexier self.

Still, Daphne enjoys all the fantasy that begins after the shot kicks in and says that Dan joins in her fantasies, talking "dirty," having kinky sex and "misbehaving" with her. She likes the fact that she can achieve orgasm a little more quickly now, too.

"Last month, I was overcome with my sex drive—so consumed that's all I thought about. This month I can control it a little better. It scared me at first that I was completely uninhibited. I wanted to explore new sexual locations like different parts of the house, in the car, with the bedroom drapes open, hoping a stranger is watching. I wanted to have oral sex in the car. Then, when the shot wore off, I was afraid to go in front of the windows where we had had sex, because I didn't want my neighbors to see me. I felt like ducking down when we were in the car. When I am in that fantasy mode, I lose my inhibitions. Dan would sit me on a cabinet and perform oral sex on me, or we would have sex in a chair with me sitting backwards.

"The first month I called the doctor's office, worried. His nurse said first-time testosterone patients often call because they are disconcerted by their driving sexual hunger. She said it's normal and told me that if it gets out of control to call again and they'll cut back on the testosterone."

Daphne has been through the testosterone peaks and valleys and says she is not scared anymore. She is just very careful when her kids are home from college. She believes that the combination of hormones prescribed for her early menopause have improved her sense of well-being, gotten rid of her headaches and other menopausal symptoms, and invigorated her marriage.

"My sex life is better than it ever was. I've never experienced anything quite like it!"

11. Is sex a function of the brain, the body, or our hormones?

All of the above. As Dr. Stephen B. Levine, a psychiatrist and specialist in sexual problems, wrote in his
book *Sex Is Not Simple*: "Desire, arousal, orgasm and
emotional satisfaction are ... sexual functions that reflect the health of our bodies, minds, and relationships."

We learned from Daphne what her sex life was
like when her female sex hormones became depleted
and how testosterone-replacement injections super-
charged her sex drive. We know that Jessica's infatuation sent her sexual juices running. Kate clearly
conveyed her inability to have a satisfying sexual
relationship because of early abuse and discussed her
recovery with hormone therapy. Sexual function is
complicated. It is scientifically understood that even
the way in which our hormones surge through our
bodies involves complicated signals between the brain
and the body.

12. *What makes penetration hurt now?*

This may well be caused by the fact that you are experiencing a lack of lubrication and a thinning and
drying of the vaginal canal, which can make penetra-
tion painful, even impossible. Sometimes the vagina is
so dry that the penis can actually cause small tears in
the tissue. This problem can be a symptom of loss of

estrogen at menopause. If so, it is easy to solve. Hormone replacement therapy can help bring back your natural lubrication. Estrogen cream applied vaginally is used by many women who cannot or who choose not to take oral, transdermal, or injected estrogen because less estrogen is absorbed throughout your system when it is applied vaginally. A number of vaginal moisturizers are available over the counter. Popular brands include Gyne-Moistrin, Replens, and Astroglide (which surely must have been named by a committee of men!). First, however, it's a good practice to check with your doctor to make sure that your problem is caused by a lack of estrogen at menopause before you decide how you want to fix it.

13. *What are the sex hormones?*

As described in Chapter 2 in "The Anatomy of Sex," the primary female sex hormones are estrogen and progesterone, and women also have a small, yet important, amount of the male sex hormone testosterone. From puberty to menopause, estrogen and progesterone are released in a cyclic fashion from the ovaries as a result of a complex series of signals from the pituitary gland (located within the brain) to the ovaries. Small amounts of testosterone, significant in governing sexual desire, are produced in the adrenal glands and the ovaries. Men have between ten and twenty times more testosterone than women: their primary sources of this hormone are the testes and the adrenal glands. In men, testosterone is also the hormone that incites sexual desire and stimulates their erection and ejaculation capabilities.

14. Will hormone replacement enhance sexual libido in women?

In his book *Sex Over Forty,* Saul H. Rosenthal, M.D., wrote that "The few women who do experience a loss of sexual desire at the time of menopause can probably attribute it to a decrease in their supply of testosterone, rather than to a loss of estrogen." It appears that although studies have shown that estrogen promotes a sense of well-being, a lack of it would dampen sexual desire only if it caused physical changes that made sex uncomfortable, such as vaginal thinning and drying. The hormone replacement that governs libido appears to be testosterone.

15. Hormones may spark sexual desire, but will they do me more harm than good over time?

That's an excellent question and one that women are struggling with all over the world, because of the pronounced lack of research into women's health issues.

The current scientific thinking appears to be that after menopause in women with an intact uterus, estrogen and progestin (a synthetic progesterone) replacement therapy (usually referred to as hormone replacement therapy or HRT) will protect us from endometrial cancer, which is a cancer of the lining of the uterus, called the endometrium. The hormones are most frequently given in the following manner: either estrogen is given twenty-five days per month and progestin is added for thirteen or fourteen days and then both are stopped for a week, or both hormones are given continuously and the progestin is given in a smaller dose. To avoid bothersome symptoms, Dr. Quigley recommends continuous estrogen—taken every day of the month—and progestin or progesterone added the first thirteen or fourteen days of the month. Women who cannot take estrogen or progestin for other medical reasons should discuss their other options with their own physicians or research alternative therapies themselves.

If a woman has had a hysterectomy with a bilateral oopherectomy (the removal of both ovaries), current scientific thinking is that no progestin is necessary and estrogen therapy (ERT) is all that is required. Progestin is the hormone that can give us the bloating and the blues, and for many women this becomes too hard to handle. There are two ways of dealing with that. Many women report real success with using natural micronized progesterone, available with your physician's prescription from the Women's International Pharmacy in Madison, Wisconsin, Belmar Pharmacy in Lakewood, Colorado, Bajamar Women's Health Care in St. Louis, Missouri, or College Pharmacy in Colorado Springs, Colorado. The 800 numbers for these pharmacies are in the Appendix.

HRT and ERT can be a blessing, preventing post-menopausal changes that can make sex uncomfortable, such as thinning and drying of the vaginal lining and frequent urinary-tract infections, as well as alleviating other menopausal symptoms—hot flashes, night sweats, insomnia, palpitations, and stress incontinence, to mention just a few of the most common. Estrogen can also protect us from the major cripplers and killers osteoporosis and maybe even heart disease and Alzheimer's Disease, which become women's health concerns after menopause.

To confound us even more, however, some studies indicate that progestin may inhibit the cardioprotective effect of estrogen. So we must become informed consumers and work with our physician/partner to balance the risk/benefit ratio for ourselves when it comes to taking hormones. Now there is yet a new wrinkle to smooth out. Testosterone therapy to stimulate sexual desire is gaining more acceptance. There are some estrogen/testosterone oral medications for women on the market today, such as Estratest and Premarin with methyltestosterone. Of course, these are all prescription drugs. Many women report excellent results from testosterone therapy, noting real improvement in their sex drives and sex lives. Testosterone injections and subcutaneous pellets (usually inserted under the skin of the buttocks) are approved by the Food and Drug Administration for use in humans, but not as libido enhancers, and work with them as libido rekindlers for women is relatively new. Testosterone replacement therapy brings with it some minor side effects, such as acne, excessive growth of facial hair, aggressive behavior, and fluid retention, so testosterone therapy must be carefully monitored. If too high a dose is taken, it can deepen your voice and also stimulate red blood-cell production, cause excessive calcium retention in the blood, and affect other diseases that you may have or medications that you are currently taking. More studies on testosterone therapy need to be done. There is more detailed information about the risks of testosterone therapy in Chapter 5.

Before you begin any form of hormone therapy, read all you can about it, ask questions, and make sure you understand fully the risks and the benefits, so that you can make the right decision about hormone replacement therapy for you.

16. I used to feel vaginal arousal during breast/mouth contact. I haven't felt that since I went through menopause. Did my parts become disconnected?

It has been said that the loss of estrogen at menopause can affect up to three hundred different body processes as well as all of the organs in the body. Since the skin is our largest organ, a lack of estrogen can make the stroking, kissing, or sucking that used to tantalize you just seem annoying. Because of lack of estrogen, you may not be feeling the same sensation or getting sexually aroused from that kind of foreplay, which may account for the fact that you feel "disconnected" from your body's responses. Most physicians explain that the nipples will continue to be sensitive and to become erect after menopause, but it may take longer to stimulate them; others indicate that there may be reduced nipple sensitivity after menopause. If a longer playtime doesn't work for you, try some new kinds of foreplay to evoke the old sensations, or consider hormone replacement therapy or one of the alternative therapies. More about both of these options can be found in Chapters 2 and 12.

17. Is it a good idea to self-stimulate, because now it takes me so much longer to reach orgasm?

Many women do just that, with their partner's encouragement. If orgasm is harder to reach, as it sometimes is after menopause when our estrogen and, perhaps, our testosterone levels have dropped, many male partners cannot delay ejaculation long enough for women to be satisfied. To increase your arousal, try setting up a sexy scenario even before you get into bed. Candlelight dinner, good music, good wine, a romantic novel, an erotic video, sexy lingerie, a warm bubble bath with cold champagne are some suggestions that might help. Fantasize. Use a vibrator to bring yourself closer to orgasm before your mate joins in the foreplay. That way you can determine when orgasm is inevitable and with practice can work toward a mutually satisfying conclusion to the sex act. Whether you achieve orgasm first or your partner does, or whether you both achieve those relatively rare simultaneous orgasms is unimportant so long as you both are enjoying sexual satisfaction. Work together at making sex work. Timing is everything!

18. Since menopause, I'm not interested in sex. I'm worried about my husband, though. Do men have to have intercourse at least once a week after the age of fifty to retain their sexual capacity?

Throughout this book, we will return to the "use it or lose it" concept of sexual activity. It is true for both

men and women that being sexually active keeps our
sex organs in good shape and retains our sexual capacity. In their 1966 landmark book, *Human Sexual Response,* William H. Masters and Virginia Johnson,
indicated that most men over the age of sixty need to
ejaculate once or twice a week. In their new book, *Heterosexuality,* written with their colleague Dr. Robert C.
Kolodny, they write, "In general, we have found that
the need to ejaculate diminishes with advancing age: a
man who ejaculates twice a week at age sixty might
ejaculate only once a week at age seventy-five, even
though he continues to have sexual activity as often at
age seventy-five as he did at age sixty." Dr. June
Reinisch says, "There is some indication that regularity
in sex, in ejaculation, and in orgasm for older men may
be helpful for some of them in terms of their prostate
health. Masturbation and oral sex work just as well as
intercourse. What women need to know as life goes on
is that erection, ejaculation, and orgasm are separate
functions in men. What that means is that a man does
not need to have an erection to have a very fine orgasm
or ejaculation." Perhaps you and your partner should
discuss how you both feel about sex and then determine
jointly what you want to or can do about it. It is important to overcome your reticence and discuss any differences in needs and wants with each other, with your
physicians, and, if necessary, with a good sex therapist.

19. Why is it that after menopause some women are more interested in sex and some are not interested?

All interest being equal prior to menopause, the differences afterward may be attributable to changing or changed hormone levels. Here again we're talking about estrogen and testosterone. Some women lose up to fifty percent or more of their testosterone along with their estrogen and progesterone at menopause; other women do not. Women who experience testosterone loss may find that their interest in sex has greatly diminished or even disappeared. Women whose testosterone levels have remained essentially the same may experience a heightened interest in sex, because now their testosterone is in the ascendancy, no longer balanced against estrogen, the female sex hormone. Remember, it is believed to be our level of testosterone along with other physical, psychological, and social factors, that drive our interest in sex.

20. I had a hysterectomy and both my ovaries were removed at that time, too. My libido has decreased greatly and estrogen therapy has not helped me. What should I do?

This is a common problem and one that most physicians do not bring up. According to Dr. Winnifred Cutler in *Hysterectomy: Before and After,* "Hormonal milieu is seriously altered by ovariectomy [also called

oopherectomy] and probably by hysterectomy as well . . .
we have learned that the uterus plays several roles in a
woman's sex life, influencing the health of her ovaries
and the functioning of the nervous system . . . the removal of the uterus is likely to have notable effects on
a woman's sex life." The many women who write to
me about this problem regret having had their hysterectomy, either with or without the removal of their
ovaries (oopherectomy) because their pleasure during
sexual intercourse has been significantly lessened. The
ovaries, you will recall from "The Anatomy of Sex,"
Chapter 2, are the major source of the female hormones estrogen and progesterone, and their removal at
any premenopausal age throws a woman immediately
into a surgically induced menopause. You need to initiate a frank discussion with your physician and together consider whether testosterone should be added
to your hormone replacement regimen. (If you can't
get a comfortable and candid discussion going, perhaps
you should consider seeing another physician.) Many
women tell me that within a week of adding a small
amount of testosterone to their hormone "cocktail,"
their sex drive is as good as or better than it was prior
to surgically induced or regular menopause.

21. *How do I explain menopause to my partner?*

I suggest that you explain it as simply and completely as you can. Let your partner know that this is a natural and universal transition for women, but that the way it manifests itself is unique to each woman. Explain that knowledge about this rite of passage empowers you both. Many women tell me that they often share certain short but appropriate parts of books or articles with their mates in order to stimulate good conversation. Some partners are willing to read a whole book on the subject, and after reading *150 Most-Asked Questions About Menopause,* many men call or write to me with their special male-point-of-view questions or comments. Other men are not ready to take on the whole subject of women's physiology in one sitting, so circling items and indicating appropriate passages or suggesting that he watch television segments about menopause with you can be a good way to help him begin to understand its many facets. Another good way is to encourage your mate to accompany you to one of the consumer seminars about menopause that may be held in your community. When I began to lecture at these programs, there were only two or three men in an audience that ranged anywhere from several hundred to over a thousand. Today, men who have accompanied their partners make up fifteen to twenty percent of the audiences. Many men ask explicit and important questions during and after the programs and are interested and involved. I'll never forget one man who came to talk with me after a program in Pittsburgh. "I came to apologize for all of the men who are not here tonight," he said. "Most of us know more about our cars than we do our wives." Happily, that's changing.

22. My sleep is so disturbed at night that I am irritable all day and don't view the prospect of going to bed, having sex, and drifting off to sleep with pleasure anymore. Has menopause forever changed my ability to look forward to good sex followed by sound sleep?

Absolutely not! This is a common complaint. It's often those hot flashes that occur at night, appropriately called night sweats, that are the culprit. One woman whose sleep had been disrupted by night sweats every hour on the hour said that she now understands the value of this tactic in torturing prisoners. Don't give up hope. There is help. Estrogen replacement therapy can rid us of the flashes and the night sweats, those most common of all menopausal symptoms. If estrogen is not for you, then try Vitamin E. Although its effects are not scientifically proven, it works for many women. First check with your doctor to be sure that taking Vitamin E is not inappropriate for you for any medical reasons. If all is well, start out with 400 International

Units (I.U.) and see if that gets rid of the hot flashes. If you still have some, increase the dosage to 800 I.U. Women tell me they get the best results when they take 400 I.U. in the morning and another 400 I.U. before bed. Other changes that can help with sleep disturbance include not eating late and avoiding alcohol and caffeine. Daily exercise early in the day helps, as does warm milk at bedtime. Evening primrose oil is reported to help. So is bee pollen. Relaxation therapy, massage therapy, and yoga can help. Take time to learn about herbal remedies, too. Find a trusted source of information and ask about herbs such as chasteberry, black cohosh, dong quai, passion flower, motherwort, and valerian root. Remember, however, that herbs are powerful. Learn about how much of them to take and what existing medical conditions you have or what medications you are taking that would make it unwise to take them. Also look into other Chinese herbs and to homeopathy as sources for solutions to your sleeping problem. Again, I caution you to go slowly and learn about dosages and contraindications prior to trying them. Sweet dreams!

"I've also learned the easier a change is to make, usually the less it matters, and that the older we get, the harder it is to choose change, which makes it even more necessary to do so from time to time. Change is one form of hope."

—Linda Ellerbee
Move On—Adventures in the Real World
Putnam, 1991

Questions for You

1. Did you know that menopause may be a marker for a reduced interest in sex?

2. Were you aware that hysterectomy and/or oopherectomy can cause sexual difficulties for some women?

3. Are you taking herbal remedies to help with menopausal symptoms?

4. Are you taking estrogen or estrogen/progestin therapy?

5. Were you aware of the role testosterone plays in our sex lives?

How Do I
Avoid Sexual
Boredom?

JESSICA ENCOUNTERED AN OLD FRIEND who became a new lover; Sallie and Don reignited their sex lives after freeing themselves from the confusing haze of responsibilities and denials that were suffocating them; Dani found excitement high on mountains, beneath the sea, and with new young temporary relationships; Kate found it in her new relationship after psychotherapy and hormone therapy. These individuals all have one thing in common: They all experienced an awakening.

The awakening can occur in spite of our current culture, which bombards us with sexual imagery and sexual gadgetry. It is no wonder we worry that sexual pleasure isn't happening as often in our bedrooms as we might like or expect when we see it exploding in books, magazines, movies, theater, advertisements, and on television daytime and nighttime soap operas. That's part of the problem: We're surrounded by sexual symbols, but we still can't talk about sex openly or well. There is no real consensus about exactly what constitutes sexual satisfaction, yet there is a yearning for it. Witness the unbelievable success of Robert James Waller's *The Bridges of Madison County,* a small book with a simple story about an erotic romantic interlude that touched the heartstrings of men and women everywhere, and of its all-too-similar sequel, *Slow Waltz in Cedar Bend.* Waller undoubtedly found our Achilles heel.

Turn on your computer to one of the interactive programs and there, on one of the bulletin boards, you'll find women and men looking for love and romance across cyberspace. Some even connect and appear on one or another national television talk shows. I recall seeing three couples, all of whom met on Prodigy, discussing their wedding plans on *The Montel Williams Show.*

When the birth control pill sparked the sexual revolution more than thirty years ago, it also spawned an ever-growing industry devoted to sexual healing. The number-one problem driving people to sex therapists is loss of libido—lack of desire for sex. Impotence clinics promising confidentiality and results are springing up all over the country. This may be because the baby

boomers are not satisfied with the fact that their en-
croaching age is bringing with it waning sexual powers. Remember, this is the generation that expanded
forever the outer limit of middle age, extending it as
far as our good health lasts. This is also the generation
of the high-powered two-income family with the jam-
packed days and nights that leave little time or resources for sexual encounters—let alone satisfying ones.

"Did I rush through life and give up good sex, so
that by the time I grew comfortable because of my accomplishments, good sex gave me up?" Don asks.
"Working seventy-five hours a week took its toll—so
did the martinis I needed in order to quiet myself
down at the end of the day."

The stress, the anxiety, the fatigue, the work, the
family, the financial pressures, and the nonstop in-
volvement with other outside activities are sure-fire sex
squelchers. Sexual interest is centered in our brains and
is bathed by our hormones and transmitted to our bodies. When we are too busy to create sexual intimacy
nurtured by love and expressed through pleasure, we
run into trouble. Then along comes the normal aging
process: menopause for women—sometimes bringing
with it vaginal atrophy and slower arousal time—and,
for men, sometimes slower and less rigid erections and
delayed ejaculations, so we've got some minor mal-
functions. But we forget that that's how we age. What

we remember, and want to have continue forever, is automatically-turned-on, top-flight sexual functioning. So we're ashamed and embarrassed to discuss sex when it doesn't work quite right (remember Sallie and Don, who weren't able to eject the elephant from the middle of their bed until she took action and they communicated?). Illness can also play a role in diminishing sexual prowess, and that should be checked out as well.

On the anniversary of the attack on Pearl Harbor, December 7, 1992, the cover of *Newsweek* proclaimed The New Middle Age, picturing a frenetic man, a Dick Tracy look-alike, with his hand on his perspiring forehead and a cloud of words covering his hair that announced, "OH, GOD ... I'M REALLY TURNING 50!" The fifty was in red and, whether preplanned or not, the article began on page fifty. Although the issue preceded the leading edge of the baby boomers by four years, it was filled with words and phrases like "balding, paunchiness, losing sex drives and capabilities, back trouble, headaches, high cholesterol and high blood pressure ..." Yuck!

June M. Reinisch, now director emerita of the Kinsey Institute for Research in Sex, Gender, and Reproduction, gave aging a new perspective. In the *Newsweek* article she asserts, "We're now seeing that 50 means all kinds of very vibrant, alive, sexy, dynamic people." Let's all shout a cheer for that!

23. How can I reawaken my sexuality?

Remember that sex sits between our ears. So if you are desirous of reawakening that sleeping giant, you'll want to learn why you no longer think sexy. You might begin by having a physical examination to make sure there's no lurking illness that is dampening your libido. Make sure you have your hormone levels checked, too. Perhaps menopause has robbed you of your testosterone as it does some women in whom testosterone levels drop as much as fifty percent when their ovaries stop production. A little testosterone replacement may recharge your sexual battery. Or maybe it's not hormones that you need. Maybe you're not feeling sexy because you're not satisfied with how you look. So look at yourself in a full-length mirror—naked! Turn side to side and front to back. Are you comfortable with what you see? Have you exercised to keep firm? No, I didn't say thin, I didn't say perfect, I just said firm. Often, satisfaction with how we look adds to our sense of sexy self, and the sense of control that comes with eating nutritious meals and performing a regular exercise program does wonders for feeling really good about ourselves. (There is more information on nutrition and exercise for self-esteem and good sex in Chapters 10 and 11.)

Now, begin to plan for satisfying sex. Create a sensual atmosphere. When we're middle-aged and in a long-term relationship, sex doesn't just happen, but it often occurs after a romantic interlude that can begin as early as breakfast that day, after a soothing massage or a bubble bath for two, or as late as midnight during an explicit video or a sexy movie. So go to the video store and rent *Last Tango in Paris, 9 ½ Weeks, The Girl in a Swing, Damage* or any one of the *Emanuelles,* or read an erotic novel such as D. H. Lawrence's *Lady Chatterly's Lover* or *The Lover* by Marguerite Duras. These movies and books have turn-on value for many women. Give sex the time, give it the proper place, and provide the right scenario, and you can reawaken your sexuality.

24. Sex for me works fine functionally, but it's kind of routine—even boring. Any good ideas?

Remember Woody Allen's 1973 movie *Sleeper,* in which his futuristic version of technosex was the Orgasmatron: You entered a chamber for simulated sexual intercourse and orgasm and you exited with a satisfied smile on your face? It, too, appeared to work functionally, inasmuch as it brought about orgasm, yet it was devoid of romance. Sounds to me like you need to get some romance into your life and to experiment with some new routes to sexual pleasure. Sex therapist

David M. Schnarch, Ph.D., author of *Constructing the Sexual Crucible: An Integration of Sexual and Marital Therapy,* is quoted in the newsletter "Contemporary Sexuality" (April 1993) as saying, ". . . people can have orgasms at relatively low levels of emotional arousal and meaningfulness. Because of its focus on dysfunction, sex therapy has overlooked the many 'normal' people who have utilitarian desire and boring-but-functional sex; there's almost no focus on helping people reach their sexual potential." So it seems that orgasm-producing, boring sex can be a problem for many people of all ages and that sex therapists don't reach out to us to help us reach our sexual potential. Even young men and women have to work toward getting their sexual selves satisfied.

For example, let's look at a sex survey created and reported by *Mademoiselle* magazine in June 1993. I deliberately chose this survey of 2400 of the very young— single men and women between the ages of eighteen and thirty—to see how and whether we change our sex act as we age. From the survey we learn that 50 percent of the women and 60 percent of the men say they don't get enough sex. One-third of the women compared to 4 percent of the men say they rarely or never have an orgasm during sex. They list their favorite kind of sex as intercourse (60 percent), oral sex (31 percent), and masturbation (8 percent). Almost half said they would enjoy sex more if they lost weight and liked their bodies better. Sounds to me as if not much changes as we age.

Shouldn't we work to increase our ability to understand what we need and want and to learn how to get it? We have to work at achieving exciting sex.

25. *Is there any way I can tell in advance whether my sex drive will diminish as I age?*

Probably not, and aren't you glad? Since this is of interest to you, however, I suggest you read about how our bodies age and learn and perfect those lifestyle changes that can keep you in good health—good nutrition, exercise, and elimination of substances that can diminish our good health and our sex drive, such as smoking or excessive use of alcohol or other drugs.

26. *I'm not as thin as I once was and my skin feels "spongy" to me. When I am undressing, I often think about how I used to look and how I wish I looked. What techniques can I use to feel pride in my middle-aged body, so that I can enjoy sex more?*

Advertising has programmed us to yearn for the lean, hard bodies of twenty-year-olds. As we learned from the Mademoiselle survey in the answer to Question 24, body image is a problem even for the twenty-year-olds.

Regardless of age, these body-image and self-esteem issues cut right to the heart of many of our sexual problems. Rita Freedman, Ph.D., author of *Bodylove,* wrote: "Body image is generally positive when self-esteem is high, regardless of a person's actual appearance. A positive body image seems to be an important component of aging successfully."

What you need to do is try to be the best you can be. If "spongy" skin bothers you, exercise, give up the fat in your diet, or consider cosmetic surgery if you think that surgical intervention will, while altering some part of your body, also improve your body image. Before you opt for cosmetic surgery, however, consider your goals, make sure that they are realistic, and ask yourself whether cosmetic surgery will fulfill them. If you still wish to go that route, take the time to research carefully to find the best practitioners in the field and check out some of his or her recent results. Remember that the brain and testosterone inspire sex. Maybe, without drastic changes, you can alter your image of your body and accept and be satisfied with yourself. There is nothing wrong with trying to improve yourself, but if that translates into negative impact on your sexual enjoyment you have to tighten the tummy or accept the image. If you've gone the testosterone route, Dr. Quigley suggests that your doctor "can encourage harnessing the extra energy provided by the testosterone replacement therapy for use in a regular exercise program to firm up." Exercise can be forever: If you've never exercised before, check with your doctor and start slowly.

Jessica told me once that after she was widowed, she was happy not to have sex and not to show her middle-aged body to anyone. Now, she confesses, from the first night with her new lover, she has never given a thought to how her body looks. When you are in love, having the perfect body really doesn't matter—having the perfect partner does. Don't diminish your present sex life by dwelling on your past or present looks!

27. I am a recent widow and have no partner, nor do I want a life partner at this time. What can I do for sexual expression and satisfaction?

Having sex does not necessarily mean engaging in intercourse. Many women report achieving satisfactory sexual expression through masturbation. Masturbation is not uncommon and is enjoyed by women as part of their sexual practices even when a partner is available. Physicians assure us that there is nothing wrong with masturbation (even though many of us were erroneously programmed to think otherwise). Indeed, masturbation is to be desired over unsafe sex. In addition to satisfying us sexually, masturbation can be a way for us to learn what kinds of touch and techniques excite us—especially if our body's sensitivities have changed. Masturbation also can be a tension reducer and a sleep enhancer in addition to keeping our sexual anatomy in good shape. In Chapter 12, you will find a number of techniques for solo sex.

28. I am quite satisfied with hugging, hand-holding, and occasional kissing. My husband says he is satisfied as well. Is there anything wrong with our leaving our sexual selves behind?

Sexual abstinence is not a problem for couples who agree to it. A number of recent studies show that celibacy in marriage is not unusual, but few people are aware of how prevalent sexless marriages are in today's society. According to Joan Avna Medicott, coauthor with Diane Waltz of *Celibate Wives: Breaking the Silence,* celibacy in marriage has multiple causes that include differing sex drives, a troubled relationship, or an ill mate. The authors estimate that 15 to 20 percent of married couples are celibate or have been at some time in their marriage. A 1990 survey of 1,500 households by the University of Chicago reported that 9 percent of married people were celibate. Single men and women also choose celibacy. In "The Men's Column," columnist Neil Chetnik *(The* [Cleveland] *Plain Dealer,* August 29, 1993) describes "the deadly dance" of empty sex and tells of a forty-five-year-old Seattle man who chose celibacy to end the dance and to learn to relax and enjoy both women and men better as friends. During my interview with psychiatrist Stephen Levine, he explained that "sex is contextual. For some of us our private internal struggles determine the context and make us say that we don't feel like making love. For others it is the interpersonal context . . . for a few people it is the biological context. We may far overestimate the power of testosterone in 'fixing' [our desire], because the personal, the interpersonal and the cultural context is much more powerful than the biological context."

29. What is a woman—premenopausal, in her early forties, and divorced after twenty years of marriage—to do about sex when she has no partner and misses having one?

Solo sex is a good way to keep you sexually active and fulfilled as well as to keep your sexual self functioning well (see Chapter 12 for more about masturbation). Next, you need to begin to seek a new partner, since that's what interests you. So many satisfying lifelong matches are made by family, friends, and coworkers that it is a good idea to let people know you are interested in dating and to accept their invitations to meet a blind date. It is important, too, if you are looking for someone with similar interests to your own, that you look for him in places that interest you—the theater, ballet, good restaurants, the symphony, western line-dancing lessons, ethnic restaurants, the bowling alley, a cooking class, at the tennis court or golf club, at church or synagogue, or at a great books study group, to cite a few examples. Taking classes and going back to school, if you have time and can afford it, is another good way to meet new people of all ages, and travel is a marvelous way to enrich your relationships. Once you meet, remember that sex has to be safe (more information about safer sex is in Chapter 13).

30. *I have no interest in sex at all, but I think I should. What can I do?*

Obviously, it is your ambivalence that is worrying you. That is not an uncommon situation. First of all, rule out any physical problems by having a physical examination complete with a blood test to check your hormone levels. If you're low on or out of testosterone, the male sex hormone that creates libido in both men and women, you may wish to discuss testosterone replacement with your physician. If that is the case, replacement will undoubtedly rev up your libido. If your hormone levels are okay or if testosterone replacement doesn't help to normalize them, remember that anger, depression, anxiety, and stress can also deprive us of our interest in sex. You may wish to seek the help of a qualified therapist. The names of several organizations that can help you locate a sex therapist or a sex counselor in your area are located in Appendix D.

31. Is there any truth to the "use it or lose it" philosophy when it comes to sex?

This is the phrase that haunts us. Clearly, physically we "work" better when we use our bodies for the functions for which they were intended. For women, our vaginal tissues lubricate better and we maintain the integrity of our body structures when we use them. For men, there is often a faster rise to erection and ejaculation and enhanced ability to repeat both more often when sexual intercourse is fairly regular. As Dr. June Reinisch comments in the answer to Question 18, "There is some indication that regularity in sex, in ejaculation, and orgasm for older men may be helpful for some of them in terms of their prostate health." Dr. Estelle Ramey cuts to the bottom line on this subject. "Use it or lose it certainly is true. The vaginal tract is less moist after the menopause; even with estrogen replacement therapy there is some diminution in the vaginal secretions. It's interesting to note that the vaginal mucosa, if it is stimulated [rubbed], increases its secretory rate, so the more intercourse you have, the easier it is to have it. This is true for women who are not on hormones as well. If they have some lubrication and, perhaps, add an artificial lubricant and have relatively frequent sex, their vaginal mucosa will not atrophy [dry] as fast."

32. Does the frequency of sexual intercourse have an effect on sex hormone balance and its possible effect upon libido?

Not really. "Use it or lose it" applies, but not to the point of being able to alter our hormone levels. For most women, our female sex hormones are kept in balance, ebbing and flowing throughout our menstrual cycle in our childbearing years. Then, as described in Chapter 2 in "The Anatomy of Sex," after menopause, those hormones diminish and usually disappear. With them can go up to half of the male sex hormone testosterone, which is produced by the ovaries and by the adrenal glands. Frequency of sex does not affect hormone balance, but hormone balance does affect the desire for—and often the frequency of—sex.

"But if I had to leave, I would. And it still wouldn't be because of a man. It would be if I started to feel that rote feeling again, that death-in-life feeling. Now I feel like I'm alive and sexual and true, and that's how I am."

—Dalma Heyn
The Erotic Silence of the American Wife
Turtle Bay Books, 1992

Questions for You

1. Have you had a full medical checkup recently?

2. Are you satisfied with your appearance?

3. Do you eat nutritious, well-balanced meals?

4. Do you follow a regular exercise regimen?

5. Is your sex life boring?

CHAPTER 5

What Can I Do to Increase My Interest in Sex?

❦

IN THE SEX SURVEY I CONDUCTED, 58 percent of the women indicated that they would like to find out how to increase their interest in sex, and 62 percent were interested in finding ways to increase their sexual satisfaction. Yet when respondents were asked to rate the importance of sex in an intimate relationship, sex was rated number six, ranking lower than love, friendship, companionship, emotional satisfaction, and romance. Sex, however, came before passion and before financial security—which interestingly and surprisingly ranked eighth and last.

According to the survey, increasing libido and gaining greater sexual satisfaction were desirable but not overriding factors in a productive relationship. Still, inasmuch as it's an important component in a relationship, let's look at various ways to stimulate our sex drive.

If you want to increase your interest in sex, you have to start out by learning how interest in sex is stimulated physiologically and psychologically. It is believed that testosterone is the androgen hormone that stimulates libido in both women and men. Some women have virtually no testosterone and some have a lot. Why the difference?

Dr. Ramey explains, "Sometimes it depends on how fat you are, because fat tissue also makes sex steroids [hormones]. Fat makes a little estrogen and a little testosterone, which is why some fat women often don't have hot flashes during the menopause. There are two things that fat is good for: One thing is that fat women probably don't get osteoporosis [as often] because bones respond in their activity to pressure and fat women put a lot of pressure on their bones; the other is that fat tissue makes some estrogen-like compound. After menopause it can compensate for the loss of hormones."

If your testosterone level is low, your answer may be to add a small amount of the male sex hormone to your hormone cocktail. Discuss this with your doctor. You may wish to begin your search for increased interest in sex with a blood test that can measure the amount of testosterone that is circulating in your blood. However, it is a fairly expensive test and the information that would result would lie in a narrow range and may not be definitive. You may want to discuss the practicality of the test with your doctor, who may suggest skipping the test and starting you on a small amount of testosterone to see what it does for you.

Studies have shown that estrogen replacement can enhance mood and reverse vaginal dryness, which may contribute to comfortable sexual functioning and improve libido. Water-soluble lubricants can also help with lubrication and there is a whole shelf full of fairly new products in the pharmacies, such as Gyne-Moistrin, Replens, and Astroglide, which were mentioned earlier. Estrogen combined with testosterone has been shown to benefit women with decreased libido, particularly following surgical menopause, according to one Canadian study.

All women do not experience a decrease in sexual activity or desire after menopause, but, according to Dr. Ramey, some 30 percent of women do. Menopause is also the time (the average age when menopause occurs is 51.4) when many other psychological, cultural, economic, and interpersonal factors come into play. Some of these are sexually liberating; some can be threatening. For example, no more menstrual mess or cramps, no more fear of an unwanted pregnancy, and grown children no longer underfoot can make sex more interesting, accessible, and unconstrained. On the other hand, aging or ill parents, empty nest syndrome (or the reverse, when the kids come back home to you, sometimes bringing their kids); illness or the loss of a partner, personal illness, and many other factors can result in anything from sexual turnoff to sexual devastation. Some couples make an appointment at a clinic similar to the Center for Marital and Sexual Health in Cleveland. As Dr. Levine explains, they come in because "it's a mystery that they've lost their sexual desire. They come here for us to decode the mystery. It's rare that we can't find a cogent explanation."

Remember, as well, that some men experience their own midlife changes. Your mate may feel insecure because it takes him longer to get an erection and he is unsure of its lasting power, as well as of when and whether he will ejaculate. His sense of machismo may depend on his continuing to "own" a seven-inch erect stalk of steel that performs at his bidding. His concern can impair his performance and send his level of performance anxiety skyrocketing. As a result, he may avoid sexual encounters. His change in interest can diminish yours as well, especially in a relationship where he usually made the first move. Is he suffering male menopause—or, as some call it, viropause or andropause? These questions are now being studied both here and abroad. Some physicians are still saying that there is no male menopause; others disagree. Who knows?

During my interview with Robert Butler, M.D., chairman of the Department of Geriatric Medicine at the Mount Sinai School of Medicine, New York, I asked whether there is a male menopause. He said, "Absolutely not! I don't think that there is any evidence for it. In the first place it's a terrible use of the English language, because menopause means the end of menses and men never had a menses! It's illogical. There are psychological things that men go through that are sometimes referred to as male menopause . . . but that's a psychological matter. Lastly, it's quite certain from the Baltimore Longitudinal Study on Aging, for example, that there are not traumatic drops, but rather gradual changes in testosterone as men grow older."

Whether or not there is a male menopause is a moot point for some physicians. Dr. Levine says, "We can give a man an erection and give the couple a good reliable penis; what we can't do is give the couple the motivation to use it." Even if the physical side of things is okay, many people still need help.

Most agree, however, that if we are healthy, good sex can last into our eighties or nineties—perhaps not the same sex as in our earlier years, but darned good sex nonetheless. A problem exists only if our demands exceed our abilities. Our job is to learn how our bodies age, learn about normal genital aging in our partners as well as in ourselves, and communicate, communicate, and communicate.

Most people don't communicate. Here are a few of the comments from the women who participated in the discussion groups that I conducted about midlife sex:

"I was bed-dead for almost the whole seventeen years I was married. I tried going back to school, but I was so frustrated that I fell in love with all my professors. I stayed in that marriage so long because I come from the kind of family where no one ever gets divorced," admitted Connie, a petite, pretty, and perky Catholic.

"I walked out after twenty-five years when the kids were in their twenties. I knew after the first week that my marriage held nothing for me and that I had come full circle—from nothing to nothing," revealed Angie, her feistiness sobered by her words and her attractive features contorted in pain. "My husband brought me a present once when I told him I was leaving. A Sony TV. I really could have used a vibrator better."

"I had sex, but I was too numb for the adventure, or the fun, or the true pleasure. Now I yearn. Can you even imagine going through life and never satisfying any sexual yearning?" Paula, a willowy, recently divorced high school teacher with two teenage children, questioned softly.

"Do you know you can be talked out of good sex by your parents, who terrify you into being a good girl? Their greatest desire was for me to be pure," Alex, still gamine and glamourous, interjected, remembering the "wasted years."

"I married someone with no urges whatsoever," Paula added.

"I didn't like my body much—I was always trying to cover it up. I tried to talk about it once, but he didn't want to talk. He said, 'What's the point?'" Connie blushed. "We were a bad match. I think he was as lonely as I was."

Wasted years. Wasted yearnings. Too little information and too little communication. Now some of us want more and better sex. Other women are happy to put an end to the sexual search and settle down to celibacy: "There's a calm that comes with that," Nancy, a chic commercial artist in her forties, revealed.

Angie, sipping white wine, vehemently disagreed. "I'm a very sexual person and my needs are great. When I was married, when I wanted it I could have it. I'd just reach over and touch his penis and it would rise. That was nice, but I'd never marry again for want of it. I couldn't be celibate, but I don't want anyone asking me where I'm going, when I'm coming home, or even where I was."

These women demonstrate varying degrees of sexual interest and sexual need. What they all have in common is that they have gathered to discuss the mysteries of midlife sex, love, and intimacy. They all want to know how to maintain or increase their interest in sex as they age. Even Nancy, who says that she enjoys celibacy, wants to know more about sexuality in case her last "great passion" just happens to come along.

I learned a lot about testosterone replacement from M. E. Ted Quigley, a reproductive endocrinologist in La Jolla, California, with whom I lectured. Dr. Quigley, one of the pioneers in testosterone replacement therapy, credits Robert Greenblatt, M.D., with being the "father" of testosterone replacement therapy for women. "I talked to Dr. Greenblatt for two hours and he changed my life," Dr. Quigley said. Dr. Greenblatt also changed Dr. Quigley's practice of medicine. Dr. Quigley had just studied twenty-five oopherectomized women (women whose ovaries have been surgically removed) using a 1–10 scale to estimate their libido and their quality of life. "Even with oral estrogen replacement therapy, most women were under 5 in terms of quality of life, and were saying, 'Something is still missing.' They had no reserve energy, libido, or quality of life!" He measured their serum testosterone and found it to be very low. When he replaced the testosterone every woman reported a quality of life score of 9 or 10. Dr. Quigley told me that Dr. Greenblatt reassured him about his results by telling him of his similar results when he had given women testosterone replacement therapy. "I began working with testosterone therapy for women because I wanted my patients to feel better," Dr. Quigley stated.

33. *Which hormone creates sexual desire?*

Testosterone is a male sex hormone that creates sexual desire in both men and women. A product of the gonads and the adrenal glands in men and of the ovaries and the adrenal glands in women, testosterone is produced through a complex interchange between the pituitary gland in the base of our brains and a man's gonads and a woman's ovaries.

34. *Isn't testosterone a male hormone?*

Yes, it is, but it is one that both men and woman have to a greater or lesser degree, and it is the hormone that spikes sexual desire. Although testosterone and androstenedione, two of the chief androgens, are produced mainly in the male testes, they are also manufactured in a lesser amount by the female ovaries and by the adrenal glands in both sexes. When replacement testosterone is given, women receive a much lower dose than men. For example, Dr. Quigley may give a woman a portion of a 75 milligram pellet, while a man may get 15 to 25 pellets, depending on his weight.

35. *What are the dangers of testosterone therapy?*

Testosterone replacement therapy is a relatively new practice. According to Dr. Quigley, in the male it may cause a cancer that is lurking in the prostate gland to begin to grow. It can also cause changes in serum cholesterol levels, raising the "bad" LDL cholesterol (the one that takes cholesterol from the liver to the cells of your body, where it can form pockets of plaque) and causing the "good" HDL cholesterol (the cholesterol that carries excess cholesterol from the bloodstream to the liver, where it is excreted) to drop. It can be harmful to the lining of the blood vessels. It may cause high blood pressure. As a result it may increase the risk of cardiovascular disease. Or it may not. A surprising finding was reported in *Arteriosclerosis and Thrombosis,* a publication of the American Heart Association (May 9, 1994). As reported in *The New York Times* (May 10, 1994), Dr. Gerald S. Phillips of St. Luke's–Roosevelt Hospital in Manhattan is the chief author of the study, which challenges the belief that testosterone is implicated in causing heart attacks in men. Two other smaller studies also have shown that testosterone may help avert heart attacks. The exact mechanism by which normal levels of testosterone may protect against heart attacks is not known at this time. So another long-held scientific belief is under scrutiny.

In women, side effects may include acne, usually around the mouth; peach fuzz and hirsutism, which is the excess growth of hair in normal and abnormal places; and aggressive behavior. More important, it can also cause a change in the voice and, like a prepubescent boy, a woman may find her voice cracking and deepening. Voice change is *not* reversible, so if the voice starts to be affected, therapy should be stopped right then and there and reevaluated, says Dr. Quigley. Male-pattern baldness can also be a problem. Dr. Ramey reminded me again of the rule in endocrinology: "If you have a significant amount of hormone circulating in the blood and add some more, you don't get much of an effect. If there's just a little and you add a small amount, it works." This means that you need to be low on the hormone for the therapy to help.

36. *How long has testosterone therapy been used for women?*

Dr. Quigley dates his work back to the early 1980s and the work of Drs. Robert Greenblatt and Christopher

Longcope to even earlier. Although physicians have made brief forays into replacement testosterone for women for the last few decades, no work of any real size and scope precedes the last twenty years. Yet Dr. Ramey recalls that about forty years ago, at the University of Chicago, work with testosterone in women won the Nobel Prize. Physicians there had given huge amounts of testosterone to women with breast cancer, having learned that the male hormone antagonizes the circulating estrogen that can encourage the cancer. That is when doctors learned that testosterone also stimulates libido in women. Back then, in the 1950s, only a handful of sophisticated physicians gave women testosterone for libido, and of the few women who took it, some were sensitive to testosterone and experienced facial hair growth. The scientists had not yet solved that problem, when, in the 1970s, along came the scary reports linking estrogen with endometrial cancer. When physicians discarded estrogen replacement therapy, they also threw away what they had learned about testosterone therapy for women.

37. *How long has testosterone therapy been used in men?*

In *Sex Over Forty,* Saul H. Rosenthal, M.D., medical director of the Sexual Therapy Clinic in San Antonio, Texas, explains that when he went to Harvard Medical

School in the late fifties and early sixties, nothing was taught about sexual dysfunction or its treatment. In 1970, when he became interested in treating patients with sexual dysfunction, it was "a very daring thing to do." Remember, William H. Masters and Virginia Johnson's landmark book, *Human Sexual Response,* wasn't even published until 1966. It opened the floodgates, but the information only trickled in. Any large-scale work with testosterone replacement is a product of the 1980s at the earliest. Dr. Ramey reminds us, however, that in the late nineteenth and early twentieth century, a doctor in Vienna made a fortune transplanting monkey testicles into men to rejuvenate them. And long before that, in many cultures, the victors ate the testicles of their vanquished foes in order to gain their power. "For more than five hundred years, men have been searching for aphrodisiacs, and in every culture you could get rich if it became known that you had a compound that would allow a man with waning sexual powers to get it on," she said.

38. *What are the results and the side effects of taking testosterone?*

Let me answer that by sharing the experience of a couple I interviewed in San Diego. I'll call them Myrna and Saul. Saul was Myrna's second husband. She had been married for twenty-two years to her first husband, had borne three children, had had an asexual relationship with her husband the rest of the time (her choice), and had gone through a bloody divorce. She then met and married Saul, who coaxed her into fairly agreeable sex which gasped and then died after her menopause. Myrna went to Dr. Quigley. He prescribed testosterone in the form of a pellet placed under the skin of her buttocks every three months. According to a smiling Myrna, she had her first orgasm after menopause!

Today scientists and physicians from many disciplines are trying to define the exact relationship of testosterone to a woman's sex drive and are studying its effect on maintaining bone density and muscle mass, as well. There is no scientific consensus on the wisdom of giving postmenopausal women small amounts of testosterone along with the other hormones, estrogen and progesterone, that are being replaced. This is an uncommon practice in the United States, although doctors in Australia and Great Britain are more willing to counter flagging libido and fatigue with a little testosterone. *The New York Times* (May 3, 1994) reported that "Dr. John Studd of the department of obstetrics and gynecology in Chelsea and Westminster Hospital in London said that besides estrogen-replacement therapy, about 25 percent of his postmenopausal patients receive testosterone pellets inserted under the skin. Dr.

Studd reported that the pellets clearly helped his patients. 'They may have their lives transformed,' he said. 'Their energy, their sexual interest, the intensity and frequency of orgasm, their wish to be touched and have sexual contact all improve.' "

Testosterone can recharge the sex drive of women who have lost it and can invent it for women who never had enough drive to begin with, claims Dr. Quigley. He also notes a remarkable improvement in energy level and a reduction in headaches, both complaints of many postmenopausal women. Dr. Ramey agrees, calling testosterone "... a great little hormone for limiting fatigue and headaches." But testosterone can also bring about the side effects described in the answer to Question 35. It is important that you discuss the risks and the benefits of testosterone with your physician, because any hormone therapy must be carefully evaluated in each individual case.

39. How is testosterone given to women?

Testosterone can be given by injection or through pellets placed under the skin, usually of the buttocks. It does not work as well when given as an oral medication because it is metabolized (changed) by the liver as it circulates through it and is short-lived in its active form. For example, Estratest, an oral medication that combines estrogen and testosterone, is prescribed on a daily basis or, if less is desired, may be given every other day, with estrogen given alone on alternate days. Its dosage cannot be individualized as easily as injections or pellets, according to Dr. Quigley. Physicians tell me that they often will start with the injections so that they have an easier time adjusting the dose to the individual. Injections' effects last from two to four weeks (you may recall that Daphne's sexual fantasies subsided and released her from her sexual frenzy the last week of each month). The pellets, which are about two-thirds the size of a dime, usually last three to four months. Myrna told me that she can tell exactly when her pellet is running out, and she runs in to have a new one implanted. On the 1–10 scale that Dr. Quigley uses, the women using testosterone report a 10 in total quality of life, while with estrogen alone, the highest he has recorded in women whose ovaries were removed is a 7.

40. How long does it take the testosterone therapy to work?

The women whom I interviewed in South California indicated that the testosterone injection kicks in in about forty-eight hours; the pellet may take four to five days. All of the women that I spoke with were keenly aware of when their medication souped up their sex drive and when it began to diminish, they slowed down. My interviewees were delighted with this change in their lives and, although some were displeased with the need for facial waxing or electrolysis to remove the unwanted hair that can be a side effect of testosterone therapy, they were happy to make the trade-offs and, as most of them put it, ". . . to get back to me."

41. *Do men lose testosterone at midlife in the same way that women lose estrogen and progesterone?*

Most scientific research indicates that testosterone levels in men decline after the age of twenty, but that they decline very slowly. So midlife male problems are not often ascribed to "male menopause," if there is one. Indeed, the physiology of normal male aging shows no shutting down of any hormone as occurs with women at menopause. Yet midlife men often suffer lack of libido, fatigue, irritability, anxiety, and, some report, a phenomenon akin to the hot flash and the night sweat. Dr. Robert Butler told me that chronic alcoholism is a major cause of low testosterone levels and that we have a very serious alcohol problem with ten million hardcore alcoholics in the United States alone. So alcohol may be a factor as well. Now a study in England by Malcolm Carruthers, M.D., medical director of the Hormonal Healthcare Centre, of four hundred men in viropause shows that there may, indeed, be a male menopause incited not, as was originally thought, by a lack of testosterone, but by sex hormone–binding globulin, which makes the body resistant to its own testosterone. After ruling out prostate cancer, which can be stimulated to grow by testosterone, Dr. Carruthers sometimes gives oral testosterone supplements to lower men's globulin levels. For other men, he uses the testosterone pellets implanted under the buttock tissue, which release the hormone slowly over a six-month period.

This process, yet to be reported in a major medical journal, may cause a skeptical "raised eyebrow" reaction within the United States medical establishment and elsewhere.

Yet Dr. Ted Quigley readily agrees with the idea of testosterone replacement for men. He has a number of men in his practice who were brought in by their wives to increase their sex drive, hoping to match their own recharged sexual vigor. "I initially worked with the men only when their wives insisted," Dr. Quigley said, so I talked to Myrna and Saul again. Yes, Myrna had insisted that Saul see Dr. Quigley. Saul assures me that his fatigue has disappeared and that his interest in sex has returned full-blown. They both smile like co-conspirators when they describe their sexual needs and how they fulfill them.

"A woman may develop wrinkles and cellulite, lose her waistline, her bustline, her ability to bear a child, even her sense of humor, but none of that implies a loss of her sexuality, her femininity."

—Barbara Gordon
The Quotable Woman
Running Press, 1992

Questions for You

1. Are you interested in learning more about testosterone therapy?

2. Are you using vaginal moisturizers to help with lubrication?

3. Are there signs of "male menopause" in your partner?

4. Do you suffer from fatigue?

5. Are headaches a problem for you since perimenopause or menopause?

CHAPTER 6

What Are
Some Routes to
Sexual Arousal?

LAST FEBRUARY, a month after my book tour for *150 Most-Asked Questions About Menopause* ended, the producer of a long-lived and very successful morning talk show in Detroit invited me to do a repeat performance on *Company*. This time she invited me to speak on a panel with Helen Gurley Brown, the chic and successful editor-in-chief for the last quarter century of *Cosmopolitan* magazine. Would I return? Absolutely!

Helen was on tour with her new book, *The Late Show,* and it was my delight to meet the author of a book written many decades earlier—*Sex and the Single Girl*—that had permanently changed the lives of many young women, giving them permission to compose and conduct the male/female relationships in their lives. I respect the fact that throughout the years Helen had held fast to her point of view. We sat in front of the audience as she struck her familiar chord. Perched on her chair, Helen told women to listen to their men, to hang on to their words, to look up to them, and then, perhaps they could cling to them in life and hold on to them until death. I looked out at the audience, mostly well-dressed women between the ages of thirty-five and sixty, and gauged their interest: Some agreed with Helen, who spoke in her delicate and endearing way. Others with perhaps more feminist leanings looked confused. Then a petite blonde with long ponytail seated in the second row mouthed the words, "Give me a break," and I knew it was time to bring a contemporary theme to the gathering. It was a terrific show!

I suppose years ago there was a fairly common belief that women had to learn how to catch and hang on to their men. Some women were actually marched off to college to get their MRS. Degree! And the fable continues: If we were lucky and hung on tightly enough, we could all retire to our rocking chairs together. Not this decade of women! We rocked and rolled right past those chairs and into bed, where active sex lives still awaited us. *The Janus Report on Sexual Behavior,* which polled 3,260 adults in a national survey, reported that 53 percent of the men and 41 percent of the women aged sixty-five and older were enjoying "reasonably active" sex lives.

The report noted that some of life's earlier distractions—children, work schedules, and the like—were diminished and that lovemaking, though perhaps less frequent, was also less hurried and more gratifying. As we've learned from the experts, if your sex life has been good, there's no reason to stop as you age, although you may have to change your tempo somewhat. The asexual elder is a stereotype that needs to be eliminated. The notion that aging must reduce sexual satisfaction is a myth. Just recall Jessica and her new lover!

According to physicians, senior adults may experience a diminution of sexual interest and response. Women can experience flagging desire, vaginal dryness, and pain. Men may find themselves unable to attain or hold an erection, and both sexes may encounter difficulty or an inability to achieve organism. But there are physicians and medications to help with these eventualities. There is also a whole fleet of psychiatrists, psychotherapists, sex counselors, and sex therapists who can deal with disturbing psychological problems—everything from fear of impotence to lack of self-esteem and distorted body image.

Now that Phil, Sally Jessy, Geraldo, Oprah, and other television talk show hosts have opened the floodgates of sex talk, we are getting more courageous about looking for help with our sexual problems. However, the biggest problem continues to be that although you can watch all the talk shows, it's hard to talk about your own sexual problems with your physician. I don't mean to knock your doc, but I do wish more of them would raise the subject and make it easier for us to get help.

In the last chapter, the comments from the discussion group—contemporary, well-educated, articulate woman all—are sad commentaries on how many women live lives of "quiet desperation." And it is no different for women from any other walk of life or from any particular region of the country. I know— I've talked to thousands of women: nurses, nannies, waitresses, cooks, attorneys, architects, and all kinds of medical professionals. The surveys, the questionnaires, the interviews, and the conversations cast a wide net. Think back to Sallie and Don in Chapter 1 and recall how she had to angle for an opening to get help with her sexual problems and how loath Don was to get help with his. According to Dr. Ramey, sex problems are even harder on the males. Women, she told me, can give up their sexuality and maintain their femininity. Unfortunately, men have been socialized to believe that their whole masculinity is compressed and rolled up into one five- to seven-inch firm rod. If they feel this way, it is a real torture when things go wrong.

42. I have totally lost my sex drive. What are the benefits of using dual hormone therapy—estrogen and testosterone?

The benefits can be great. For some women, it takes just a small amount of testosterone to perk up their dragging sex drives. Some postmenopausal women report a real boost with Estratest or with one of the other oral medications such as Premarin with methyltestosterone, which combines estrogen with testosterone. Several physicians suggest starting slowly to see how the testosterone affects you. Dr. Hanna Lisbona, my own gynecologist in Cleveland, suggests that women try the combination pill for about thirty days. See what it does for you and whether you get any of the undesirable side effects. The dose can then be adjusted accordingly. Dr. Ramey believes that only women on estrogen should consider taking testosterone, because it is the estrogen that will protect them against any testosterone-induced changes in their circulatory system that can be harmful.

A 1993 Gallup poll surveyed 705 women and found that 71 percent reported no change in their interest in sex since menopause. Dr. Ramey indicates that 30 percent of postmenopausal women have a declining interest in sex after menopause. Another Gallup survey of 833 women between the ages of forty-five and sixty was sponsored by the North American Menopause Society (NAMS) to ascertain the respondents' knowledge of and experience with menopause. That survey revealed that only 16 percent of the respondents knew anything about combined estrogen/androgen therapy, demonstrating clearly that all options are not being outlined for women by their doctors. According to Isaac Schiff, M.D., chief of gynecology at Massachusetts General Hospital and a past president of NAMS, "Many women may feel intimidated about discussing intimate concerns with their physicians, particularly about sexuality and emotional changes." Isn't it about time that doctors helped us to be the best that we can be? If they don't raise these important issues for us, we had better take charge and ask the right questions ourselves!

43. Is testosterone replacement therapy approved by the Food and Drug Administration?

According to Dr. M. E. Ted Quigley, the Food and Drug Administration (FDA) has approved testosterone for use in humans who have low testosterone levels. The FDA stated: "We have no drugs approved for enhancing libido in women. Estratest is an exception that's pre-1962 or, at least, pre-1970 and that's why it's there without scientific data." So some of the others such as Premarin with methyltestosterone are sometimes prescribed for libido, but they are being used "off-label," meaning they are not being used for the use for which they were indicated or approved.

44. I'm fifty-five and sexy. My mate is a slug. In males, do certain health problems or diseases cause sexual impairment?

They can. The list is wide and long. Diabetes and hardening of the arteries may impair sexual performance, as can many medications such as those taken for high blood pressure, anxiety, and depression. Prostate infection and urinary infection, among other illnesses, can cause sexual problems. Perhaps he is experiencing a midlife crisis having to do with his work or another aspect of his life that is causing him fatigue, or perhaps he is anxious about his ability to get and sustain an erection. Other psychological problems, even stress from family matters, can make sex a luxury that he doesn't allow himself. I suggest a good physical checkup to rule out illness and to see whether your doctor can't help to put sizzle back into your sex life. If your partner feels uncomfortable bringing up the question of sexual impairment with the doctor, suggest that he write down what he wants to know on a three-by-five index card and read it to the doctor verbatim. It will get that important discussion going. Writing down your questions about sexuality is a good idea for women who also find that conversation uncomfortable.

This is a time for communication, understanding, and a thorough medical checkup. If your mate is interested in checking into testosterone therapy, he can discuss this controversial treatment with his physician and learn the facts and weigh the risks and the benefits. This is your time to be informed, patient, and helpful.

45. *Is there an increased risk of cardiovascular disease with testosterone therapy?*

Yes there is, and Dr. Estelle Ramey explains it this way: "Back to the rule in endocrinology: If you have a significant amount of hormone circulating in the blood, and you add some more, you don't get much of an effect. If there's just a little and you add a small amount, it works. So, if women have little or no testosterone and you replace it with a small dose they will feel better; more interested in sex. But the proviso is that they had better also have estrogen to protect them. If not, they're setting themselves up for long-term troubles in terms of heart disease. As for men, if they already have a lot of testosterone receptors and they're all filled up and you give them a little more testosterone, it's like putting an electric blanket on a dead man—nothing! So in order to gain an effect you have to give a lot. That's dangerous! Testosterone is an androgen, and the problem with these androgens is that they have a very profound effect on every other tissue in the body, including the blood vessels and the heart. That's why men die earlier than women. Giving more testosterone to men increases their risk of heart disease. It can also adversely affect the liver. It may mean that we'll usher them out a little sooner!" Whether or not to even consider testosterone replacement is a subject for discussion with your physician. In *The Kinsey Institute New Report on Sex,* Dr. June Reinisch wrote "... current medical thinking is unless a man's testosterone level is tested and found to be exceptionally low, there's no benefit in adding more [testosterone] and there may be negative mental and physical health-related side effects." It seems important that men be depleted in testosterone before it is prescribed for them and that testosterone therapy is carefully monitored. A man or a woman with personal or family history of heart disease may not be a candidate for testosterone replacement. New research is underway. Dr. Quigley says that work with hormone replacement has to proceed slowly. You have to fine tune—one hormone at a time. See Question 35 and talk to your doctor!

46. *What are vaginal moisturizers?*

There is a whole fleet of new water-soluble preparations that can improve vaginal lubrication, such as those I mentioned earlier—Gyne-Moistrin, Replens, Astroglide, and numerous others. These are available over the counter and women tell me that they are very effective. Some women use them daily, others, two or three times a week. Many women add this extra form of lubrication when estrogen replacement therapy does not seem to return their vaginal lubrication to a comfortable level, although most doctors assure me that that shouldn't be necessary and that perhaps these women need to discuss with their physicians the options of increasing the dosage of their estrogen or changing the form of estrogen that they are taking. Nonetheless, if you are experiencing vaginal discomfort such as dryness or itching and you've checked with your physician to make sure there is no other problem, vaginal moisturizers can be a blessing. Increasing your sexual activity, if possible, can help greatly, too.

47. *Do sexy videotapes help, and what is the difference between pornography and erotica?*

This is a question that comes up repeatedly in conversations after the seminars and in notes to me on the survey sheets. To get the best answer I went to the *Journal of Sex, Education and Therapy* of the American Association of Sex Educators, Counselors and Therapists, Volume 19, 1993, and to a study by Richard M. Saunders, B.A., and Peter J. Naus, Ph.D., which was designed to examine the difference in the effect, if any, upon men and womens' sexual identity, behaviors, attitudes, and values when they viewed erotic and pornographic sexually explicit videos.

It was noted that earlier studies of erotic and pornographic materials had shown "inconsistent" results. Some showed that pornography produced antisocial behavior; others indicated that sexually explicit materials can have "positive, attitudinal, and behavioral effects." In fact, it had been reported in earlier work by M. Yaffe in his "Commentary on Current Trends in Sex Therapy" in *Current Trends in Treatment in Psychiatry* (published in Bath, England) that earlier researchers W. C. Wilson, J. H. Gagnon, and W. Simon had found that "sexually explicit materials have a definite place . . . in sex education and therapy and . . . a positive role to play in the prevention of sexual problems." It is interesting to note that in 1980, leading feminist Gloria Steinem was among the first to differentiate between pornography and erotica, considering "dehumanizing" materials and those "having little to do with sex and much to do with violence and subordination" as pornography and "mutually pleasurable sexual expression between people who have enough power to be there by positive choice" as erotica.

The study by Saunders and Naus, which used commercially available videos, demonstrated that erotic film segments elicited different perceptual and emotional reactions than the pornographic segments. The pornographic films were perceived by the participants in the study as more exploitive and degrading and, thus, produced an overall negative effect on the participants. The reaction to the erotic films was that they could contribute to sexual pleasure.

48. *How do I create the right atmosphere for successful sex?*

Setting a sexy scenario can begin at breakfast. Creating intimate conversation over mimosas, cappuccino, and croissants with a bouquet of violets on the table can begin the day in a close, sensual manner. Eliminate points of controversy or argument and present loving thoughts to each other. As the day unfolds, flowers, perfume, a cozy fire, interesting reading material that you might share passages from, and music that you both appreciate can help to make the day one for loving each other. If possible, make sure that any others who live in the house are away. Disconnect the phone, ignore the doorbell, run a bubble bath for two, or massage each other with perfumed oils. Whatever works for you both is what creates your own sexy atmosphere. I know one woman who only feels sexy in a black lace teddy; I know another who gets her kicks in a large T-shirt with the Teddy Bears' Picnic silk-screened on the front. One woman gets turned on when her partner wears black briefs: another is set aquiver by semitransparent silk trunks. Creating a sensual setting is an area where your creativity can be allowed to run wild. If you haven't experienced creating a sexy scene, try it. You might find it especially exciting!

49. *How do I think sexy when I don't feel sexy?*

Remember that sexual desire is a product of the brain, the body, and our hormones. In fact, the brain is our most exquisite sex organ! You need to take the time to discover why you don't feel sexy. Are you feeling fat? Get on a good exercise program and let those happy endorphin hormones, which are released when we exercise, work for you. Endorphins can make you feel up, while you're trying to bring your weight down. Take control at mealtimes by limiting the fat in your diet. Being in control is a powerful feeling. Are you feeling ugly? Get a new flattering haircut, a manicure or pedicure, a facial, a makeup makeover, or buy, create, or concoct a new outfit. Make a list of what has worked to lift you out of your sexual doldrums in the past. Then go for it. Read a romance novel, take out the erotic videotapes, take a luxurious bubble bath, reread the answer to Question 48, and have fun.

50. Do you think dressing the part of a sexy siren helps to enhance sexual arousal?

For some people that works. If it works for you, do it. Sometimes putting on your sexiest underwear, your slinky black dress, your highest heels, piling your hair into an updo, and making up your best face is like a tonic. Or dress up like your favorite fantasy—from parlormaid to naked nymph wrapped in diaphanous scarves. There is nothing wrong with dressing the part you want to play as long as it pleases you and gains the desired effect from your lover. Angie, a member of our discussion group, is seeing a married man who occasionally asks her to dress up for him in a black garter belt and high heels. She says, "If he likes my middle-aged jiggling body that way, it's okay with me as long as he doesn't ask me to do it too often."

51. I fantasize a lot. Is that normal?

We are told that 90 percent of our sexuality is in our minds and, thus, the images in our minds play a vital role in enabling us to become sexually aroused and to enjoy our sexual experiences. Therefore, sexual fantasy may well be universal. Women's fantasies may be more romantic, but often they can be wild and crazy as well. Fantasy can be a normal and wonderful part of our sex lives. Fantasy is only a problem when we deal with socially unacceptable fantasies and act out those fantasies. We can get into big trouble that way. As children, our fantasies may have helped us learn through compromise how to solve problems or to handle situations that were not to our liking, and this may work well for us throughout life. In his book *Sex Is Not Simple,* Dr. Stephen Levine has written that "the sexual fantasies of orgasmically inhibited women are especially interesting because they provide clues to their requirements for arousal and to the sources of their inhibitions. Some fantasy themes recur over and over for decades and seem absolutely necessary for orgasm." Fantasy can satisfy our wishes, calm our fears, and bring us satisfaction in the form of making things or people—even our partner—into whatever or whomever we wish. It's our own private playground!

"Desire is appetite with consciousness thereof."

—Baruch Spinoza
Reflections and Maxims
Philosophical Library, 1965

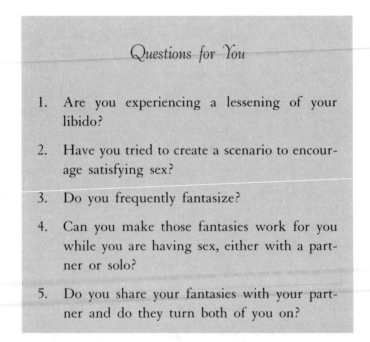

Questions for You

1. Are you experiencing a lessening of your libido?

2. Have you tried to create a scenario to encourage satisfying sex?

3. Do you frequently fantasize?

4. Can you make those fantasies work for you while you are having sex, either with a partner or solo?

5. Do you share your fantasies with your partner and do they turn both of you on?

CHAPTER 7

Why Don't We Just Talk About It? Improving Sexual Communication

SEXUAL WANTS, needs, desires, and changes are still taboo subjects to many people. They're hard to talk about and if you're unaccustomed to discussing sex with your partner, you have to couple that taboo with another fear—the fear that you'll say something that will turn your partner off. Deborah Tannen's bestselling book, *You Just Don't Understand,* has enjoyed particular success because she's told us how he hears what you're saying and vice-versa.

A good example is a relationship in which she asks repeatedly, "Do you love me?" and he responds, "I married you, didn't I?" That's not what she wants to hear; that's not what she is asking for. Reassurance in more concrete terms is necessary. Or what of the woman who envisions slow, luxurious caresses and kisses in a loving and sexual encounter that is in tempo with her slower arousal time, but cannot discuss this with her mate in a way that is not critical of him. If you want the best sex, you and your partner had better learn how to become the best communicators! Dr. Reinisch calls communication "the best aphrodisiac . . . the best lubricant!"

Kate, Wilma, and Mary think sexual communication may be easier in a lesbian relationship because such a relationship often begins with and continues to have better communication. Feisty Angie once confided to our discussion group how she "blew away" her third marriage. She explained that she and her husband were from diverse backgrounds, had different goals and different needs, and that there was no way to make the marriage work—except that she loved having sex with him. Well, one night, she confided, she had this fantastic orgasm and after it was over, she said, "Is that all there is to us?" He packed up and left her two days later. "That was probably a good thing," she said, "although I was surprised I said it, because when I'm thinking about screwing, I'm not usually thinking about loving. There's a big difference between the two, and just good fucking doesn't sustain a long-term relationship, I guess."

Casey, married nineteen years to her second husband and one of the more conservative members of the group, raised the issue of love in response to Angie's comments. She asked the group, "What does love mean to each of you?"

Angie shot back. "I don't believe most people know what love means. Do you want to know what those words mean to me? They mean I come first and if a man says he loves me, I want him to mean he understand my appetites, whatever they are."

"Wouldn't it be even better if someone just has the desire to understand those appetites?" Casey countered. "I don't think that any man can understand or acquiesce to what's really important to us."

We went around the room trying to define love, only to realize that we each brought a different definition to the table. Maggie wondered if men really want to have a life with someone—to be in any kind of a relationship. Paula wanted her mate not to pay attention to anyone but her. Angie said that maybe her ex loved her as much as he could, and she admitted that she thought she loved him too, but at that time, she thought, she didn't have a clue as to what love was all about.

Round and round the discussion flew, leaving some of the group agitated as hell, until calm, clear-thinking Dani offered a definition that we could all accept:

"When I was married, the Unitarian minister who united us defined love for us as *"active goodwill."*

We were awestruck. We were silent. Then we

cleaved to her definition and went round and round again, each attesting to the fact that the person from whom we felt love and to whom we gave it unstintingly was our best friend first.

The sex survey bears out our small-group finding. The questionnaire asked that eight qualities be evaluated and ranked in terms of importance to us in a relationship. Love outranked everything else, gaining 47 percent of the number-one ranking. The qualities valued second and third were friendship (21 percent), and companionship (18 percent). There was then a drop to 12 percent for emotional satisfaction and a drop to 6½ percent for sex, 3 percent for romance, and ½ percent each for passion and for financial security.

In the survey, similar qualities such as friendship and companionship were listed separately so that the results would allow for differences in interpretation of those words. If the concepts of friendship and companionship had been lumped together, then the total would have almost equalled love and paralleled the minister's definition that appealed to all of us.

As hard as it is to talk about love, talking about sex is even worse. Think of your mate as a man whose masculinity may exist in his penis and then try to tell him that something he is doing isn't working for you. Kapow! It's rough, but if you can lay a good foundation for good sex communication, you've got a chance.

Maggie, one of the widows in our discussion group, claims that her current live-in lover is her best friend. "Finally! I can say anything I want to him and he can do the same. He's open, he's secure. He had a couple of bad marriages, he's a recovering alcoholic and a staunch member of Alcoholics Anonymous. He did enough suffering of his own and he puts a high value on me and on *us.*"

Connie disagreed vehemently. "It's not that simple! I think it all depends on what kind of a family you had. If you've come out of your family with your self-esteem intact, then you're fine. If not, until that's in place you'll never know what love is and you certainly can't communicate about sex."

Beyond considering it active goodwill, we never did figure out how to define love, nor did we develop a formula for communication about our sexual needs. What we finally agreed upon was that with effort each of us can build our self-esteem and begin to love ourselves. Once we do that, we are able to love others. When we love, we can communicate with hope rather than with anger. This type of loving communication will enable us to enjoy more satisfactory sexual activity.

52. How do I explain to my partner about my night sweats and sleepless nights and my need to be left alone sexually?

Give your partner this answer and ask him to read it. The night sweat is the twin of the hot flash, and they can begin as early as in your thirties, even when you are still menstruating. Day or night, they can be severe for some women, awakening them many times at night and causing major disruptions in their lives—particularly in their sex lives.

Night sweats can make you slippery, the bed soggy, and your sleep disordered. Then you carry your tired self into the busy day, with disastrous consequences. These nuisance symptoms of changing hormone levels are caused by a change in the chemistry of the brain that affects the thermostat in the hypothalamus, lowering your body temperature set point and causing the blood vessels of your skin to dilate. Then you sweat as your body attempts to reset your thermostat.

Relief for hot flashes and night sweats usually comes with hormone replacement therapy (HRT) if you have your uterus intact, or estrogen replacement therapy (ERT), if your uterus has been removed. Not interested in, or cannot take hormones? Then try Vitamin E. It can work wonders for many women, eliminating flashes and permitting sleep. Start with 400 International Units (I.U.) in the morning and, if necessary, add another 400 I.U. at night to combat those flashes and sweats, but to be on the safe side, check with your doctor first. Try herbs and other alternative therapies too.

Now that you've explained to your partner that sometimes you don't feel like "hot stuff," you can try to eliminate the night sweats, improve the quality of your sleep, and get on with a hot sex life.

53. How do I manage my sex life when my partner and I have different goals? I like to cuddle, he wants to come.

It is not uncommon for women to desire more loving touch and more caressing than men, and some even tell me that the most satisfying prelude to sleep for them is to curl up with their back to his front (or vice versa) like spoons and drift off to sleep enraptured by the warmth of the hot breath on their neck and the naked skin wrapped around and behind or in front of them. But spooning is not known to be one of man's great sexual pleasures and although he may be willing to engage in cuddling as the foreword or the afterword, for him the main text is sexual intercourse or oral sex and the climax, quite frankly, is his climax. You need to have a frank discussion about the fact that you love having sex, but that you also adore relating skin-to-skin sometimes with no conclusion except a cozy warm way to drift off to sleep. During the intensely cold winter of 1994, NBC Tonight's Jay Leno quipped, "It was so cold in Minnesota that men were actually hugging after sex!"

54. How do I get my partner to understand my sexual needs?

This is a question posed by women of all ages, but particularly by those at midlife, when it may take us a little longer to get aroused, to lubricate, and to achieve orgasm. This is where intimacy enters into that loving relationship. You've got to talk to each other about how our bodies age and what we can do to make those changes positive ones. For example, if you need more stimulation, ask for it. If you need extra stimulation—explicit videos, bringing a vibrator to bed with you, even talking "dirty," discuss it. Explain that this is not a reflection on him, but a change in you. You know that by the time a man reaches forty, he will have had at least one experience in which he failed to get an erection. Then it's your turn to be understanding and find new routes for arousal for him. You may have been able to fake sexual pleasure at some time during your life, but no one should have to fake it, and at midlife you certainly can't fake sexual intimacy. This is a time to help each other out, so that you can continue to have a satisfying sex life.

The politics of "orgasm for all" requires trial and error and good communication. If you are able to discuss your needs, make certain that your words cannot be construed as criticism of him, but rather as an explanation of what you need. If you cannot say the words, then perhaps you can let your partner know by small groans of pleasure what feels good. Or you can gently move his hand or his mouth in such a way that it covers a different area or deepens pressure if that is what you need. Many women with a problem similar to yours use a vibrator in preparation for sex and even during foreplay and sex in order to help themselves arrive at orgasm, while their partner is still erect. Remember, it is one of the great myths of all time that mutual simultaneous orgasm is the objective of good sex. It happens rarely.

55. When I sneeze or cough, sometimes I wet myself. This sometimes happens to me during intercourse or during orgasm. Now I'm afraid to relax and enjoy sex. I feel so embarrassed when this happens. What can I do?

It sounds like you're suffering from stress incontinence—a condition many women loathe talking about. For some women, it's taboo! Yet you must talk about it with your doctor. Stress incontinence involves the leakage of urine when there is pressure on the bladder. This happens when the sphincter muscles to the bladder get too weak to hold in urine under stress. Child-

birth, loss of estrogen, and age can stretch those
muscles and weaken their "hold-in" power, so pressure
from sports, sneezing, even laughing hard can cause a
little leakage of urine. Don't be embarrassed to seek
help. You are not alone. This is a problem for "40 percent of women who are 60 years of age and older," says
T. Franklin Williams, M.D., director of the National
Institutes of Aging in *Healthline,* a publication of the
National Institutes of Health (NIH). In most instances,
stress incontinence can be controlled and sometimes
cured. Start doing Kegel exercises. Those are the ones
in which you loosen and tighten your pelvic muscles
(they are described in detail in Chapter 11). Kegels
help many women tighten the pelvic muscles, which
can help contain urine and keep it from being released
from the bladder under stress. There are estrogen receptors on the sphincters, so the HRT or ERT also can
be most helpful in alleviating this problem. Nonsurgi-
cal and surgical procedures are available which may
help you. Don't suffer and don't ruin your sex life
worrying about this. See your gynecologist or a urologist and find out what kind of help is available. Many
women tell me they would be much more comfortable
discussing this with a female urologist—which hereto-
fore has been difficult to find. Luckily, it is now possible to write to Dr. Jean Fourcroy to locate a female

urologist in your area. Her address is located in Appendix D. There is a lot of work being done in urodynamics and some interesting procedures are performed using collagen injections to add bulk to the urethra. (During nonsex times and while you're getting yourself back in shape, there's always Attends, Depends, Serenity, or Poise, or you might consider using panty liners if you're experiencing only a small amount of leakage during sports.)

56. *My mate has sexual problems that are affecting me. Should I tell him?*

Yes, but be very careful how you tell him. Even in the most intimate, loving relationship, talking about sexual dysfunction can be dangerous. A man's sense of his masculinity is often wrapped up in the performance of his penis. When a man can't rise up to his promise, you may want to tell him that this happens to every male once in a while and that you really don't mind. You need to know, however, that he really does mind and that more of his masculinity than this one sex act is involved in this failure. All the hugging in the world can't make it up to him, so it's better to have an honest discussion and to suggest that he might want to have a medical checkup to make sure there's no underlying medical reason for his disappointment. Try to get him to mention this problem to his doctor and hope that his doctor is comfortable enough discussing it to offer help.

57. *What is impotence?*

Impotence is an unfortunate word. It literally means lack of power, chiefly of copulative power or virility. It is defined as the inability of the male to perform the sexual act. Getting an erection, which seems like a simple bodily act, is actually a very complicated process. It requires harmonious interplay among the brain, the nervous system, and the blood flow to the penis. Today in most medical circles, erectile dysfunction is beginning to replace impotence as a diagnostic term. That's probably a better choice of words.

58. *How do I talk my mate into going to the doctor about his problem?*

Tenderly. You might start out by explaining that there are gradual changes in sexual functioning in both men and women once we pass forty. Our reflex mechanisms may be less sharp and our hormones less ample. There are also a lot of diseases, psychological changes, and other factors, all of which should be checked out, that can alter our sexual abilities. For example, diabetes, hypertension, some medications, alcohol, tobacco, anxiety, tension, and even some nutritional deficiencies can play a role. But, according to Dr. Robert Butler, "Men have a great deal of ego and, unfortunately, they are performance-driven. They began with a kind of quantitative approach to sexuality and it is often very difficult to get them to seek help." Approaches that might work include asking your family doctor or clergyman to help or encouraging your partner to talk to one of them. All you're asking him to do is check it out—because you love him.

59. *How many men are impotent?*

Impotence affects ten million to twenty million American men; another ten million may have partial dysfunction, a National Institutes of Health (NIH) panel of experts reported. According to the NIH panel convened in Washington, D.C., in December 1992, there is no inevitability to impotence, and it is treatable. With proper therapy, men can enjoy sexual activity throughout their lifetimes. Treatment should start with a complete medical and sexual history. Modifying diet, alcohol intake, stopping smoking, and retailoring medications can help, too. The most recent and largest study of impotence (1,709 men) since the Kinsey Study was reported in *The New York Times* (December 1993), just one year after the NIH panel report. This study of men in Massachusetts by Dr. John B. McKinlay, director of the New England Research Institute, found that about half of the men over the age of forty have experienced varying degrees of impotence. This regional study suggests that nineteen million men in the United States between the ages of forty and seventy may either be impotent or have at some time experienced impotence. Impotence comes in several forms and from varied causes, both physiological and psychological. Diabetes, hypertension, and vascular disease can play a role. Medications can be part of the problem. Psychological reasons are myriad, from loss of a partner to loss of a job, from resentment to performance anxiety. This is a sleuthing job for your partner and his physician. Where to start? Probably with a good physical examination. If everything is okay, then a visit to a urologist who specializes in impotence or to a good sex therapist is in order. Irwin Goldstein, professor of urology at Boston University School of Medicine, revealed in *Longevity* (February 1994) that most age-related impotence results from reduced blood supply to the penis. "It's basically a plumbing problem," he said. Dr. Stanley Althof, associate professor of psychology in urology at Case Western Reserve University School of Medicine and co-director of the Center for Marital and Sexual

Health, explains that most men hope it is. "Men come in to see me and say, 'I want this to be physical' because for a man that means that 'I don't have to have the stigma of going to a mental health professional or a sex therapist.' " Dr. Althof added that men find it preferable to find that there is something physically wrong with them, rather than "come in the door and say I think there is something wrong in communication, or in our relationship, or there is something wrong from my childhood that is now getting in our way." Several first-rate organizations that can help you find a professional in your area are listed in Appendix D.

60. *My husband heard something about penile vacuums on the radio. What are they?*

A penile vacuum is an ingenious device that forces blood into the penis, causing it to become erect—or bringing about a semi-rigid erection—rather quickly. It works this way: A plastic cylinder is fitted over the limp penis and then the air is sucked out of the cylinder through a plastic tube that is located at the outer end of the device by either a pump, a syringe, or by mouth. The removal of the air creates a vacuum that, in turn, causes blood flow into the penis, causing an erection. Then a tourniquet device, like a rubber band, is placed around the bottom of the shaft of the penis, trapping blood in the erection chamber and enabling the erection to last for up to twenty or thirty minutes. When the tourniquet is removed, the erection subsides. Although the success rate with the vacuum constriction device is high, it has some potential nuisance problems, such as loss of spontaneity, reduced quality of ejaculation, and even physical discomfort. There are also battery-operated devices and condomlike ones. These devices require a physicians' prescription. (For more information, contact the Association for Male Sexual Dysfunction listed in Appendix D.)

61. *What is a penile implant?*

Penile implants came into use in the 1970s. There are two kinds. One is inflatable; the other works with silicone rod-shaped forms inserted into the penis. According to Dr. June M. Reinisch, author of *The Kinsey Institute New Report on Sex,* both types have advantages and disadvantages. The inflatable implant is made up of dual silicone cylinders that are inserted into the erectile areas of the penis and are connected via tubing and a pump to a small balloon in the abdomen. When the man activates the pump that hangs in his scrotum (using a switch or handle, depending on the type of implant he has), fluid stored in the balloon fills the cylinders, causing the penis to become erect. When the erection is no longer needed, a flip of a switch on the pump causes deflation and sends the fluid back into the balloon. This inflatable implant is relatively expensive and requires surgery and hospitalization, as well as excellent operational skills by the man. Although rated to be most like natural functioning, the implant can malfunction and additional surgery for repairs may be required. The silicone implant, on the other hand, can irritate penile tissue, and although it costs less than the inflatable device and is rarely subject to mechanical failure, it may make urological examination and testing difficult. Implants can also cause infection. Silicone implants can send silicone particles into the lymph nodes, making urologists reluctant to suggest them because the long-term results of that migration are unknown, even though no problems with the migrating silicone have been clinically identified as of this writing. The problem of silicone in *all* of these devices is on an upcoming agenda of the FDA. Because implants destroy any natural erectile capabilities, they should be the last option to be considered.

62. *What are penile injections? Do they work?*

Penile injections are relatively new and are considered to be fairly safe, although some negative side effects have been noted, such as too-prolonged erection or some scabbing at the injection site. In this procedure a vasoactive drug, usually papaverine or phentolamine, or prostaglandin E, is injected into the penis using a needle and syringe. The drug causes the blood vessels in the penis to dilate and become engorged with blood. An erection is often attained in fifteen to twenty minutes or less and may last an hour. Research continues in this area. The biggest drawback to penile injections is the man's reluctance to self-inject the penis. There are a number of other new treatments in the scientific pipeline. Minoxidil cream, applied topically, and nitric oxide drugs look particularly promising.

63. What is sexual dysfunction?

In the medical dictionary, the word dysfunction is used to describe an impairment, disturbance, or abnormality of the functioning of an organ. Sexual dysfunction indicates that there are problems, of a physical, social, or psychological nature, in how we function in the sexual aspects of our lives.

64. What kinds of therapy can improve our sex lives?

After checking out your physical condition with your internist or family physician to rule out any physiological problems, the next step may be to seek the help of an appropriate professional who is an expert in dealing with sexual problems. You are probably looking for a marriage counselor or a sex therapist. If you can talk about this kind of personal problem easily, you might begin by asking your personal physician or clergyman to recommend someone, or you might ask family, friends, or coworkers who may have gone to a counselor or might know of one. You could also check with your local mental health center, medical school, or large teaching hospital. Or you could write to the American Association for Marriage and Family Therapy or the American Association of Sex Educators, Counselors, and Therapists for the names of certified therapists or counselors in your area. (When you write, ask whether there is a charge for this service.) The addresses of these organizations are listed in Appendix D.

65. My husband's sexual abilities have diminished, but he won't talk to me about it. What diseases are associated with impotence?

Impotence can be linked with diabetes, prostate infection, urinary infection, some medications for hypertension and many tranquilizers and antianxiety medications, as well as other physical ailments and medications. The list is fairly long, and that is why it is important to get your husband to his physician for a full physical evaluation.

66. *What else can I do to help my partner and myself to enjoy our sex lives more?*

Throw back the covers on pillow talk and communicate with each other more. Sex talk is never easy for some people, but it is important. You need to let each other know how you feel about sex, where you rank it on your list of favorite activities, what feels good, what's changed, and what turns each of you on. What is it that happens that causes you to be interested and to lubricate? What makes him have an erection? Too many of us quietly let our sexual interests and powers run down, rather than talk about what is changing in us and what we desire.

> "Self-expression must pass into communication for its fulfillment."
>
> —Pearl S. Buck
> in *The Last Word*
> Carolyn Warner
> Prentice Hall, 1992

Questions for You

1. Do you feel comfortable discussing your sexual needs and desires with your partner?

2. Do you and your partner understand and reassure each other when things in your life, including sex, don't go exactly as either of you wished?

3. Is stress incontinence a problem for you?

4. Is impotence a problem in your sexual relationship?

5. Have you tried erotic videos, a vibrator, or talking "dirty" to turn each other on?

CHAPTER 8

How Do I Get My Sexual Affairs in Order?

✿

THE WOMEN I INTERVIEWED all had different ideas of what they wanted sexually and of what would make them feel complete. Some, like Dani, wanted the casual sexual encounter filled with excitement and passion, but no commitment or long-term obligations. She just wanted to have good sex with a great guy and then go on living her totally independent life. She wouldn't mind, however, finding a virile, intelligent traveling companion who could carry her pack. Dani says, "That's just the way I am. I don't need to judge myself or worry about anyone else judging me anymore. When we've already developed a persona in which we're comfortable, I think that kind of carefree choice is possible."

Jessica wants love, love with passion, love with pain.

She enjoys the love when it is occurring and suffers over it during the long intervals between meetings. She wouldn't want it any other way. She says, "I'm as uncomfortable with knowing about sex as I am with understanding investments. God help the men with whom I fall in love. I could drive them nuts, because I'm so insecure."

Angie won't trade her freedom for anything, wants sex for sex's sake, and wants some help with her bills. Nothing more. She maintains that there's nothing new under the sun when it comes to sex. "At this point in my life, I don't need to be validated by a man."

Sallie wants her sex life with Don to go on as it always had. She wants her vision of the complete circle—marriage, sex, love, and intimacy, and she'll fight to maintain it.

Kate wants her life with Mary to have the best sex now that she's learned what good sex can be like—and she wants it in the context of a solid long-term relationship.

"Some women are delighted to be done with sex. They didn't enjoy it much anyway," said Nancy. "You may not agree, but I think you have your strongest sex drive when you can reproduce."

"Biology plays the leading role," added Dani. "It used to be thought that after we had our kids that we were dead as members of the species. Not anymore!"

"At this age, I'd just as soon have good friends," confessed Casey.

"I have plenty of friends; it's a lover that I need," said Alex.

"My mother told me to have an affair when I was thirty. When I was forty-six and having marital trouble, the psychiatrist friend I went to told me to have an affair. So when I went back and told him I was having an affair, he said, 'Oh, boy, you didn't get it! I meant for you to have the affair with me,'" Angie told us.

"That's so unprofessional!" came a chorus from the group.

Are affairs the answer? Shere Hite reported that 75 percent of women married more than five years had extramarital sex. Her book, *The Hite Report,* was written in 1976. Just fourteen years later, in 1990, the Kinsey Institute of Sex Research cut that number to less than half. The Institute found that 29 percent of married women had had an affair (37 percent of married men had been unfaithful). The Doctors Janus reported in 1993 that one in four women and one in three men had had an extramarital affair. So, in this age of AIDS, do the numbers of unfaithful continue to drop? At the American Enterprise Institute seminar in October 1993, researcher Tom W. Smith of the National Opinion Research Center at the University of Chicago reported from his survey of 1400 individuals that 13 percent of women and 21 percent of men admit to having had an affair. Smith, whose research conflicts with the earlier reports, adds that he estimates that three to four percent of wives and husbands have sex with someone outside their marriage in any given year. Does this represent a real conflict of numbers, or the fact that AIDS and other sexually transmitted diseases are now so prevalent? In 1994, in their book, *Heterosexuality,* Masters, Johnson, and Kolodny tell us that "extramarital sex hasn't disappeared in the 1990s." Yet the late 1994 report from the Chicago team's study published in *The Social Organization of Sexuality* reports Americans are largely monogamous. Even the experts haven't reached a consensus.

67. *Do many married women have affairs?*

As reported above, I guess it depends on whose research you believe. In *The Janus Report on Sexual Behavior,* 1993, the doctors note: "A decade after our first study, we found that fidelity was more highly valued in marriage, in what seems a significant shift for Americans." The Doctors Janus write that it is not that fidelity is more stylish, or that the dangers inherent in swapping body fluids account for the change, but rather "that marriage as an institution and a commitment to a spouse is now more highly valued." Reporting on a survey examining sexual attitudes and behaviors of 18,876 people between the ages of sixteen and fifty-nine conducted in England in 1990–1991, *The New York Times* (February 1, 1994) noted that the results surprised even the principal investigator, Kaye Wellings, a medical sociologist at the London School of Hygiene and Tropical Medicine. The results showed that the vast majority of those surveyed practiced monogamy. America and England seem to agree.

68. *Sex with a new partner is the only thing that turns me on now. Is it selfish to seek pleasure outside my marriage?*

In Chapter 7, I stressed communication with your partner to enhance your sexual pleasure. Before you seek outside pleasures, which can be dangerous to your relationship and to your health, I suggest you try to work toward better sex within your partnership. Talk to your partner. It is better to seek the help of a sex counselor or therapist than to look for sex outside your relationship. The sex survey that I conducted showed that only three percent of the respondents were engaging at that time in extramarital affairs. Many women I interviewed find a new man exciting, but rightly insist that you have to be careful and practice safer sex. It's frightening out there! Many state that they found their sexual satisfaction in the "open marriages" of the 1970s, but that they now are much more circumspect in their activities. One sexy brunette said that when she got frightened enough, she began to try and talk about their sexual problems with her mate. She was shocked and delighted when he agreed to see a marital therapist with her. Not too long ago she called and told me that she is now finding exciting sex within her marriage because she let her husband know that she felt that their sex lives had become humdrum and that she would love to have him spice it up by choosing unusual places and ways to have sex. "For example," she explained, "I was in the laundry room and he lifted me up and seated me on the vibrating dryer and began to undress and caress me. It was great! We would never have dared fool around like that before, because each of us thought that the other would be appalled at the unorthodox behavior. It's a shame that I didn't know sooner that I could be honest about my sexual needs. Once we began to work toward the same goal, our sex lives left nothing more to be desired." Working out a pattern for successful sex together may well represent the highest form of negotiation. Try it!

69. Do most women at midlife seek out younger men as sex partners?

Of the women I interviewed, age was not the issue in their search for sex partners. Jessica has a seventy-four-year-old passionate lover. There are many stories like hers, because healthy men who remain sexually active do not lose their sexual powers and may be able to summon them to a greater degree within the excitement generated by a new or an illicit relationship. However, it is usually the young men who are more likely to want to jump into bed and gymnastically display their rising passion. The May-December relationship stereotypically has referred to the young woman and older man. That is changing! I've lectured in the breadbasket states frequently, and a chic, articulate well-educated woman with whom I've remained in touch (I'll call her Barbara) has had a lover almost thirty years her junior for several years. She is a stunning fifty-five years young. They plan to marry once her divorce (which she initiated) becomes final. Barbara put me in touch with a number of women in her menopause support group who are also in sexual relationships with younger men. They all seem to echo the same sentiments: "If it's good sex that you're looking for, you need someone who would rather fuck than sleep!" Do not think for a moment that some older women are not moved by the appeal of younger men's virile bodies.

70. My bloody divorce left me gun-shy. I no longer seek marriage or even a lasting relationship. I am just interested in good sex. How do I convey my new beliefs to potential partners?

You're not alone. In their book *Our Turn: The Good News About Women and Divorce,* authors Christopher L. Hayes, Ph.D., Deborah Anderson, and Melinda Blau report that in surprising numbers women are expressing a lack of interest in remarriage. Eighty percent of women report valuing their privacy and independence. The book is based on a study of 352 women that was published by The National Center for Women and Retirement Research at Long Island University's Southampton Campus and reflects the impact of divorce on women who are forty years of age and older. In that study, the women reported a healthier sexual identity and an appreciation of the freedom for sexual experimentation.

The problem is learning how to convey this information to potential partners. The best way to do this seems to be to state the facts. In today's disease-shrouded sexual scene, there are a lot of vital negotiations that must take place before you jump into bed, such as whether both of you have been tested for HIV, who is providing the condom, what are the guidelines that you'll follow to ensure that you're having safer sex, and so on. This is also a good time to discuss the fact that you are not desirous of sex ending your single personhood, but rather complementing it. Remember Dani's lover at the campsite who entered her tent and said that he wasn't going to marry her and her retort, "I certainly hope not!" They had a great eight days.

71. I am a staunch feminist during the day, but I love to be submissive to my man at night. How do I find partners who can understand my sexual dichotomy?

You have to be willing to discuss it. Over the years men and women have confused each other and confounded themselves trying to understand their roles, whether in business or in bed. Feminism has as one of its basic tenets that women must define their own experience. To do so you must not deprecate yourself or your worth as you relate what you desire or what turns you on sexually. This "submissiveness" does not have to extend to how you choose to conduct or accept any other facet of your life. Sex is special, sex is mysterious, sex is a personal experience and one that you can define. In a *Ms.* magazine article entitled "Radical Heterosexuality," author and new-wave feminist Naomi Wolf noted, "We need a heterosexual version of the marriages that gay and lesbian activists are seeking: A commitment untainted by centuries of inequality." This is the equality of relationship that Kate, Mary, and Wilma speak of with such pride.

72. *Why is touching—soft, gentle, sexy touching—so rare?*

Perhaps it is rare because most partners don't know how to express this form of tactile sensuousness. Touching is an essential part of satisfying foreplay. It can bring some women to the brink of or even to orgasm. The epitome of this kind of sexual arousal was depicted in "The Piano," a 1993 film written and directed by Jane Campion. Neither of the film's two lead characters is the classic symbol of sexuality, yet Harvey Keitel raises Holly Hunter to sexual consciousness, arousal, and seduction in a series of prolonged touching experiences. Many men have pronounced this gem of a film as a "chick flick" or a "woman's movie" and I wonder if this is not because they are not accomplished "touchers." In our younger years, a kiss, a touch, a caress were merely preludes to sexual intercourse. They were hurried in a way that suggested "Let's get it over with and get into the main event." At midlife these manifestations of sex, love, and intimacy may be fully satisfying by themselves. Many women forget that men enjoy being caressed, too. For the men who need stimulating, inventiveness in your caressing can reap rewards. Gentle touching of his buttocks, nipples, testicles, and penis offer pleasurable sensations that may or may not lead to sexual intercourse.

73. My mate and I are changing roles somewhat. He is more nurturing and I am more aggressive now. I find this both comforting and disturbing. What's going on?

What's going on, in part, is a change in your hormones. You are probably losing some of your estrogen, the nurturing reproductive female sex hormone, leaving your natural testosterone, the male sex hormone, more unopposed and more pronounced. Thus your more aggressive self. The reverse is probably going on in your mate, as his testosterone diminishes somewhat and his nurturing self is emerging. In addition to the obvious hormonal changes that we experience, psychological changes also occur. It has been said that as we live together, couples take on some of each other's characteristics. I think this happens in long-term relationships in which we have absorbed a part of the other person's persona. Then, too, getting older for some people has value in making us more secure and more comfortable being aggressive or nurturing, whichever the case may be. We may now not feel the need to censor parts of our natural selves.

74. How do I handle getting from a dinner date into bed?

I have always been most comfortable with a softened direct approach, but that is harder today with the limitations that AIDS and other sexually transmitted diseases (STDs) have put upon us. If we want to make the dinner-to-bed transition in a good long-term relationship, then make sure that the dinner is pleasant. No talk of problems, of children or grandchildren, of house or business, but just speak of things that are pertinent to you two as a couple. Good wine, good conversation, and a good—but not too heavy—meal in an appropriately appointed setting can set the stage for good sex. If this is a new person in your life, the same scenario applies, except that you must add to that conversation the necessary information about safer sex. A friend, Leslie, recently reminded me of how the implications of that conversation have changed. Leslie has been divorced for sixteen years. About ten years ago, she met an appealing man on a coast-to-coast flight. They began to talk when the plane stopped in Houston and their conversation continued unabated until they landed at LaGuardia Airport in New York. On their second date, Tim said that he could see that they were headed for bed in the near future. He offered to show Leslie the certificate noting that he had tested negatively for

HIV and asked her if she had been tested. She was furious. "Of course not," she said. "What did he think I was—a wanton woman?" She never saw him again. Today, she readily admits that she wouldn't consider sex with anyone unless they had discussed the subject and assured each other of their clean bills of health and their promise to use condoms. Times change.

75. Should I share information with my partner about my affair with a younger friend? The little I have told him turns him on.

I would be very careful. You are better off sharing someone else's experiences from a book or a video than discussing your own. That turn-on can turn off and turn against you later. Many people tell me they get hot hearing their partner's former sexual exploits in detail. Some even practice menage à trois—sexual threesomes—but then they're both culpable if blame is to be levied later. If you have a good extramarital affair going on, it's best to keep it to yourself. Tell your partner the plot of the *Story of O* by Pauline Réage, a modern erotic classic filled with sex and violence, or pick some soft-core erotic novel.

76. I want, quite simply, to be wanted sexually not to simply fulfill a service or function, but as a person. Is that unusual?

No. It should be the rule, not the exception. People who don't mind serving a sexual function only are either sexual surrogates, hired to help sexually dysfunctional men or women, or prostitutes who perform sex for pay. Most people want to be the designated recipient of their partner's sexual desire and expression, and intimate love.

77. How do I plan for safe sex with new partners?

There's no way to do it without being prepared. One woman told me she can't believe it, but she keeps a condom in her wallet now, just like the boys did in high school and college. If you envision a time when you might be caught without having had the conversation about HIV testing, etc., then be prepared with a condom and insist that it be used. Your life can depend on your forcefulness. Once, when I was on a television show talking about my book *150 Most-Asked Questions About Osteoporosis,* the segment preceding mine was about the female condom. What an odd-looking device. It was wide at the opening, about seven inches long and tapered into a point. At either end there was a ring, one smaller internal ring and a larger external one. I remember thinking that I couldn't imagine women being that wide, putting that flimsy contraption inside themselves successfully, or feeling certain that it would protect them. Not much has been heard of the female condom lately, but that is also something you might want to explore. As odd as it looks, it is good protection. When I raised the topic with my discussion group, Maggie howled, "I understand that they cost two dollars and fifty cents each. I'd have to really want the guy desperately to spend that much on one shot!"

78. *Should I be offended if my potential partner suggests that we both be tested for STDs?*

Absolutely not. You should be flattered. It means that he thinks enough of himself and of you to want to ensure you both good and long sex lives. The issue of safer sex is not one that can be skirted any longer. The odds are too high. Actually, according to Dr. Estelle Ramey, women are more susceptible to disease than men. That is because with less lubrication to the vaginal canal as we age, we can quickly develop small tears or fissures that can collect and trap germs. Men, on the other hand, because of their "outside plumbing," have a much tougher surface over their penises and are somewhat less likely than women to become infected during sexual intercourse. All of the experts say that we can enjoy sex into our old age as long as we stay healthy. As long as we are healthy, we are not old.

"Growing old is a matter of years. You are young, and then you are middle-aged, but it is hard to tell the moment of passage from one state to the next. Then you are old, but you hardly know when it happened."

—Doris Lessing
The Summer Before the Dark
Alfred A. Knopf, 1973

Questions for You

1. Do you prefer to be in a steady relationship?

2. Have you ever had an extramarital or an out-of-relationship affair?

3. Are you having an affair now?

4. Have you ever tried to put on his condom as a part of your sensual foreplay?

5. Do you routinely practice safe sex?

CHAPTER 9

What Can I Do to Maintain Sexual Sensation?

"HE RUBBED HIS HANDS OVER ME and for the first time in my life, I felt absolutely nothing. I lay there frightened for myself and frightened for our relationship. Where did the sensation go? When did the excitement die? He was breathing a little more heavily and his breath was hot on my neck. I still felt no arousal. This was unusual. Something in his closeness, in his desire, had always aroused mine. But not tonight. His mouth was moving from my ear down my throat, over my shoulder, he was sucking on my nipple—drawing it in and out. I could feel his teeth. Still nothing. Still stone. I'm in trouble now.

"I read a sign once that said, 'If you always do what you always did, then you'll always get what you always got.' Not now. Not tonight. He's doing what he always did. I'm not getting hot, like I always got. I'm not getting anything. I've got a problem!

"That isn't how it began. I actually picked him up. It was raining hard and we were in the alcove of the mall, waiting for the storm to abate. He was all decked out in an expensive suit, shirt and tie, and carrying an eel-skin briefcase. Me—I was feeling kinda' kooky. I was so proud of my new curly wash-and-wear haircut that I offered to get his car. He didn't accept the offer, but he did invite me to have a drink with him. We waited in the bar in the Mexican restaurant, having Margaritas until the rain slowed down.

"I took him home. I got out of my tight jeans and leather boots and told him to mix drinks while I got into something more comfortable. I joined him in the den, wearing my robe and slippers. After a few sips of our drinks, he slipped his hand gently up under the robe, smiled and said, 'I bet myself that you wouldn't have anything on underneath.'

"That's how I was and that's how we met and now I'm the one reporting that my interest in sex has flown out the window. Go figure! I don't get it. I don't mind getting older. That's an obvious route that we take and I don't run in for face lifts, surgical nips and tucks, lotions, potions, or creams, but I'd do anything to get the old sexual furnace turned on." Angie's dismay blanketed the group.

Dani, widow and world traveler and now in her mid-sixties, explained almost apologetically that her sex drive had not changed. "I would say that I am as interested in sex now as I was at age nineteen. Oh, yes, the options and the opportunities are far fewer, but the interest is the same. And remember that I was pretty faithful in thirty-five years of marriage, even when I was in sexual overdrive and my partner wasn't."

It is hot that day and there are just a few of us, sitting in the living room sipping iced tea, and we're all feeling differently about sex. Dani feels the same as always, Sallie has worked through some tough problems, but now as a result of hormone therapy she and Don have reclaimed a good sex life. Angie, the sexpot among us, is bemoaning her greatly diminished sex drive, while Alex's interest in sex with a new "friend" has mushroomed. In one small group we've run the gamut.

Alex reminded us that she had lived the life of an American princess, which wasn't royal. Her parents stifled her, her husband pampered her, and she was widowed and almost sixty before she had any independence and any good sexual experiences. Dani exclaimed that one of the by-products of her widowhood was total freedom for the first time in her life. Angie would like to feel something, perhaps not what she did before, but something.

"I don't mind that things change. I'm getting older.

I would mind being blind or having a stroke, but I'm not exercised about the rest of it. I don't want to be young again, it was too tough! And if I had the same overwhelming sex drive I did as a kid, I'd be miserable at this age. I'd be too busy masturbating to go to work," said Angie.

Alex likes being her age, too. Although she's made several visits to her favorite plastic surgeon, she's delighted not to deal with periods or pregnancies. She's taken her chins up to please herself.

All of us talked about the great beauties who have a very hard time aging. "Think of Norma Desmond in *Sunset Boulevard,*" I said. "She had everything 'fixed' and still railed against the God of aging."

"Do these remodeled women think that they're going to walk into a room, and that some young thing is not going to think they're invisible anyway?" Angie asked.

Dani told of her friend—plump with gray-streaked hair—who has been going with a man for about six months and doesn't see her girlfriends anymore and has given up golf, which had been the love and salvation of her life. All of the women say that they don't know what she'll do if he dumps her. In the meantime she's the one going around with a smile on her face. Self-esteem is based on liking our own packaging, and for everyone the package is different.

Casey had been quiet. Then for the first time she shared something very personal. She recalled telling her first husband, a prominent politician, that she had met a noted personality at a meeting and he responded with, "Did you tell him who you were married to?"

"No," she replied, "I told him who I was!" Her husband didn't take kindly to that.

This chapter about sensual sensation is about self-love. The consensus of our group is that you have to love yourself before you can love anyone else. I have a friend, an eminent psychologist, who says, "People treat you the way that you treat yourself." I think he means that in every relationship you set your own value. You don't get what you deserve, but rather what you ask for. We all agreed and added that it's better in life to ask for forgiveness than to ask for permission.

We decided that men from our midlife generation still don't get it. If we show independence, we're bitchy. We're supposed to be mushy and mommy. We confuse men.

Connie said, "You know what I finally did? I picked up the television set and walked out the door. I even left my kids and isolated myself on the other side of the river. I didn't want the kids with me because I wanted to find out whether there was any self inside me at all. Then I denied finding me for a long time. I went with one man after another. Finally I stopped, and this manless time of my life is so good, because now I'm learning about me. The kids understood in time, but I wish I had been more sure of myself long ago. I would have done everything better—the marriage, the kids. Very few people have it all!"

79. *Do I need a whole hormone cocktail—estrogen, progestin, and testosterone—to return to my old sexy self?*

Let's review what these hormones can and cannot do for you in terms of your sexiness. Estrogen can eliminate vaginal thinning and drying and make sex more comfortable. It's also kind of an "upper," so it can improve your mental state, making you feel better. Further, it can possibly end insomnia, thereby elevating mood, eliminating mood swings and the minor depression and irritation that can come from little sleep or interrupted sleep. Progestin is generally prescribed for women with an intact uterus to protect against endometrial cancer, so there is no established benefit to our sex lives with that hormone. In fact, depending on how it is prescribed, for some of us it can cause a return of our periods, which can be a brief deterrent to sex for a few days each month. It can also be a "downer," giving us the blues (although for many women natural micronized progesterone can eliminate that depression. Check Appendix D for the 800 numbers of the Belmar

Pharmacy, Bajamar Women's Health Care, College Pharmacy, and the Women's International Pharmacy. All of these can, with a prescription from your own doctor, send it out to you). Testosterone is the libido instigator, bringing many women to even better than their former sexual selves. However, to protect us from heart disease as described in Chapter 5, it should be given only to women who are also taking estrogen. Dr. Quigley told me that he has given testosterone replacement to former breast cancer patients who are reluctant to take estrogen. Of course, you must discuss this option with your own doctor. An article written by gynecologist Gloria Bachman of the Robert Woods Johnson School of Medicine and reviewed in *The Female Patient* (July 1993) argues that " . . . in studies comparing women who take estrogen to those who undergo estrogen and testosterone therapy, women in the second group fared best. They have measurably improved energy levels, well-being, and sexual response without any lessening of the benefits of estrogen."

If you're interested in natural progesterone, you may want to check out Progest cream, which is made from Mexican yams. It is said that it can alleviate vaginal thinning and drying and because of its natural progesterone content may protect you against osteoporosis, but studies about it have not been published yet. There are a number of natural estrogens made from soy products or ginseng. (The testosterone pellets that Dr. Quigley uses are actually made from soy products.) There are various herbs that work, too. For example, Damiana may prompt passion. It comes from a shrub found in the deserts of Texas or Mexico. Red or purple clover, found in North American and European meadows, is said to have mild estrogenic effects and to stimulate lubrication. Vanilla beans from vines in Central America are said to stimulate male potency, but must be used sparingly to avoid toxicity.

Just as you must educate yourself about taking hormones, when you want to take the homeopathic or herbal route, it's important to learn more about the properties of these substances, and I have listed good books on each subject in the Appendix.

80. *Why does the progestin depress me and make me feel too blue to want sex?*

Progestin is a synthetic form of progesterone, one of our natural female sex hormones. For some women it's a "downer", the hormone of PMS, the blues, and the jitters. When you feel that it's hard to get up a sexual head of steam, you might want to consider talking with your physician about oral micronized progesterone or find out whether you can take progestin every other month, every third month, or every sixth month instead of each month. Studies have shown there's no magic to taking progestin each month to clean out the uterus and protect you from endometrial cancer, and many physicians have finally (at first grudgingly) given in to new prescribing regimens. Many women find less frequent progestin means less cloudy moods and more interest in sex. Dr. Quigley told me that "continuous use of HRT [estrogen and progestin] for the purpose of eliminating menstruation can make some women depressed and can have a diminishing effect on their sex drive." He suggests reducing the amount of progestin to 2.5 milligrams and the use of vaginal ultrasound to check for thickening of the endometrium.

81. *Why am I so tired all the time?*

It is not, as so many doctors tell us, because we're getting older! It may be because we've got an underlying medical problem, so check that out first. Also ask whether your thyroid gland has slowed its production of thyroxin—that could add to your fatigue, and a little extra thyroid may help. Your fatigue may be caused by excess weight, which you can drop with proper nutrition and a low-fat, high fiber, calcium-rich diet; it may be because you need to exercise and get those happy endorphin hormones circulating through your body; and it may be that a little addition of testosterone will, as many women and physicians say, help relieve fatigue. Dr. Ramey agrees that a small amount of testosterone could help lift fatigue and be harmless as long as you also are taking estrogen to protect your heart. Dr. Reinisch says, "Testosterone is probably a good thing for women to take since we were making it anyway. Those hormones are important to the entire body." Dr. Quigley's patients all agree that testosterone in small doses can lessen fatigue. Stress and a myriad of psychological problems are also fatigue causers, so if none of the other modalities work, try talking about your fatigue with a good therapist. Often very short-term therapy can help you to identify the problem and effect a solution.

82. *What kind of sexy videos can make me feel sexy?*

In the answer to Question 23, I've listed the titles of some soft-core explicit movies available on video that are the most commonly mentioned by my groups and in the surveys. There are also a whole other genre of videos that are more of a how-to approach. For example, there is a series that has been advertised in the book review section of *The New York Times* and elsewhere called *The Better Sex Video Series. Speaking of Sex* is a self-help sex education video from the Sinclair Institute, which also offers other tapes, including *Becom-*

ing Orgasmic. Playboy Enterprises offers for sale a tape titled *Secrets of Making Love to the Same Person Forever.* These tapes are not for the easily embarrassed, because the sex scenes are graphic as well as informative. Yet this new genre of videotapes have come on the market at a time when couples are investing more in monogamy and want to spice up their sex lives at home. According to Dr. Reinisch, however, most women prefer their erotic videos woven into the threads of a story. A good idea, she suggests, is to set video guidelines with your partner, discuss your likes and dislikes and give each other veto and shut-off power. Here again, the communicators do better than the strong silent endurers.

83. *How can I recapture the sexy me?*

Work at thinking sexy, looking sexy, and being sexy. Try to have sex in a different way, in a different position, and in a different location. Try the unpredictable. Read erotic passages to each other or have sex outside on your terrace, balcony, deck, or in your garden. In a long-term relationship when sex is always the same— and for many couples it is—everything may function well, but nothing's too exciting. You always know what will happen. You are now programmed to know that if he does this, you'll do that. Think back to the last time you experienced sexual expression with a new partner. Remember how exciting it was when you didn't know what would happen next or where it would happen? That was a sexy part of the whole experience. It was fun and sex should be fun! Consider how you prepared for that experience. Do you ever spend that kind of time getting into your sexy mode now? Dr. Reinisch says we all jump too quickly to sexual intercourse. We've forgotten how to play and to prolong a sexual experience, how to work up to the act with the prologue being as important as the climax. Did you know that, according to Isadora Alman, author of the "Ask Isadora" advice column, speaking on the video *Speaking of Sex,* that most sexual encounters take place in three minutes? We can do better than that, can't we? Have a long, calm, friendly discussion with your partner about what you each consider sexy. Talk about it. Work at it. Sex should be sexy!

84. *What can I do to make my mate want me?*

We all change in a long-term relationship. We take each other for granted. "He'll be there, she'll be there, so I'll do it later" can be the prevailing attitude. Also, in both men and women, our sex drives slow down. In a lucky relationship, we slow down to about the same speed. Remember, however, that in Chapter 1 we learned that men's sex drive peaks at age seventeen and womens' at age thirty-eight. That's a problem right there. Or maybe he's feeling performance anxiety. Or maybe it has nothing to do with you or with sex. Often we all take a mountain of life's problems into bed with us. That's a turnoff. Dr. Reinisch suggests this is another area where communication is the key. You must talk with your mate about your sexual needs and desires and how much you want him, but, she cautions don't ever do it in bed or in anger. I love her idea of having these kinds of "difficult sex talks" in the car, when you're out for a drive. That way you are both facing forward, have jobs to do, and can speak calmly and directly, but not eye-to-eye.

85. How is it that testosterone creates the sex drive in both men and women?

The construction of our bodies and their systems is exquisitely divined. Every part has a function and a job and so do all those hormones that are circulating in our bloodstreams. It just happens to be that the male hormone testosterone was designed to be the sex driver. It has some other functions as well, such as muscle builder and aggression instiller, and that is probably why men have between ten and twenty times the amount that women do.

86. With less estrogen and progesterone circulating in my bloodstream now at menopause, shouldn't my testosterone take over?

For those women who do not also lose some testosterone, that happens—and sex can become better than ever. In other women, 50 percent or more of their testosterone can be lost when the other hormones disappear. Ninety percent of our testosterone is made in our ovaries (the rest is produced by our adrenal glands), as is our estrogen and progesterone. If our ovaries cease functioning, it is easy to understand how our testosterone would diminish as well.

87. Is testosterone replacement therapy common?

No, and many physicians do not even make their female patients aware of the function of testosterone or discuss its loss. I think this is something that we will begin to hear more and more about as medical science starts to spend more time and money on research into women's health issues—an area that has been virtually ignored for far too long. Women also need to take the time to learn about it and request information from their physicians. Women who do take it report that testosterone has invigorated their sex drive, eliminated their heavy sense of fatigue, and, in some cases, gotten rid of their menopausal headaches.

If testosterone is of interest to you, have a no-nonsense discussion with your physician. Good information about testosterone replacement is available through the Women's International Pharmacy, 1-800-279-5708; Belmar Pharmacy, 1-800-525-9473; Bajamar Women's Health Care, 1-800-255-8025; and College Pharmacy, 1-800-888-9358. Call and ask them to send information to you and to your physician.

88. *Do most physicians know about testosterone therapy?*

The survey done by NAMS (described in Chapter 6) indicated that only 16 percent of the women surveyed had ever been told of androgen [testosterone] replacement by their physicians. This is an area in which physicians have been remiss, either through lack of knowledge themselves due to lack of scientific research, or through lack of interest. This is another area of women's health care where you must take charge!

"Perhaps middle age is, or should be, a period of shedding shells, the shells of ambition, material accumulations, ego, pride, false ambition, and one's mask, one's armor. Perhaps one can, at last, in middle age, be completely oneself. What a liberation that would be."

—Anne Morrow Lindbergh
A Gift from the Sea
Pantheon, 1975

Questions for You

1. Do you love yourself?

2. Do you treat yourself the way you would want other people to treat you?

3. Do you want to recapture your sexy self?

4. When you have sex, are you having fun?

5. Have you ever masturbated?

What Are Good Sex Signals?

❧

IS IT BODY LANGUAGE or pheromones, those chemical substances within us that send out the sex signals that say, "I want you!"? Some women can enter a room and within minutes are closeted in close conversation with the most attractive man in the room, their encounter dripping sexual innuendos that heat up the space around them. You know not to interrupt or join in. Were her antennae out for him or did she exude some magical chemical that called out to him? She's not particularly beautiful, although some may think her striking. She is well put together, but more than that, there is something in her stride and in her stance that says, "Come to me. I'm available, I'm interested, and I like you."

Her gestures are sexy; the way she throws back her

head to laugh at what's being said, the way she reaches over to pull up the shoulder of her black dress when it slips down on her arm. Even the way she leans against the fireplace and smiles up at him gives off sex signals. Her eyes say it all, and they rarely leave the eyes of the speaker, engaging his every word and making it her own. When she speaks, her voice has a creamlike quality, deep and rich and thick.

Of course there are other obvious body language giveaways like the way a woman crosses her legs—in extremis, just think of Sharon Stone in that short white dress being interrogated in the film *Basic Instinct*. The wrap of a surplice neckline, the dip of the body and the shift of concealing clothing suddenly revealing just a little more of you than was expected can titillate and pique interest. There have been numerous studies done of these forms of nonverbal communications that tell us how to send the signals that we want to send. One of the first books to send body language into the popular press was *Body Language* by Julius Fast.

Self-esteem that enables you to shoot straight to the heart of the matter can also send sexy signals. For example, the classic World War II poster of Uncle Sam, his outstretched arm and his pointing finger, and the words "Uncle Sam Wants You" beckon in a direct way! And men and women all over the United States responded. Now we're talking about making love, not war. It's like a "Your tent or mine?" question. Having self-esteem means liking yourself enough to know that you have something to give, which conversely means you like yourself enough to be able to receive and that you're self-assured enough to ask for what you need and want. That chemical attraction comes from a couple of types of chemical behaviors. There is the rush of adrenalinelike neurochemicals that is called infatuation that may last for years if you're lucky. After that there are the endorphins, which can help us maintain that loving feeling.

In our group, Dani said that by midlife we should have arrived at the persona with which we are comfortable. The discussion group agreed and echoed that we have to love ourselves before we are free to love anyone else. Once we have our self-esteem in place we can toss out the idea that our culture values only the young and beautiful, and begin to capitalize on our own intrinsic values. To understand the hold that midlife women can have on men, remember (or rent) *House Calls,* a 1978 movie starring Glenda Jackson and Walter Matthau. Matthau plays a widowed surgeon who gives up his gaggle of sweet young things, Boz Skaggs, granola, bean bag chairs, and waterbeds for Jackson, an opinionated, feisty, middle-aged cheesecake-baker and hospital admitting clerk. My favorite piece of dialogue goes like this:

SHE: Don't you sometimes wish I was younger?

HE: Hell no. I wish I was. What are you talking about? It's comforting with an old broad like you. I don't have to explain things all the time—like who Ronald Colman is!

By midlife we have experience and knowledge, and our missions, our goals, and our values are pretty clearly defined. Those are compelling and appealing qualities, if we know how to use them.

So, is sex important? A survey of 1,007 American adults conducted for an NBC television executive showed that 59 percent of women and 80 percent of men said good sex was a necessary ingredient for a happy life. (At age fifty, the percentages dropped slightly to 47 percent of the women and 78 percent of the men.) Still, in this survey, women of all ages put sex at the bottom of their list, behind health, family, religion, and money. Even so, women still want to know how to send good sex signals if and when they want a romantic interlude.

Start with the premise that things don't just happen, but rather that there is preplanning in the works. Earlier in this book, there is information to help you fulfill your desires by sending come-on sex signals to your mate. There are also suggestions for finding a new mate through family, friends, coworkers, or activities that you enjoy. The answers to the questions in this chapter are going to explain how to keep sending sexy signals once you're with your potential partner.

89. *Do you think how a woman walks demonstrates her interest in sex?*

First and foremost, I think it demonstrates her energy level. If a walk has bounce and pace, if the body is erect, the head held high, and the eyes look forward, the message is that this is a woman who knows who she is and where she is going. Her movement is purposeful. If her arms are free and swinging as she walks, she appears in a happy or contented energetic mood. All of the energy in the walk can be translated into sexual energy. When a woman swivels her hips gently as she moves, the walk is also considered sexy.

90. *My friend suggests that taking a sensual bath together or kissing in the shower sends signals that sex is desired. Is that true for most people?*

As far as I know, there's never been a study that can directly answer that question. However, many of the experts will say that sending signals indicating some sort of sexual follow-up is desired is a common prologue to the sex act. Showering or bathing together, soaping each other gently, embracing and letting the warm water soothe your skin as the soap bubbles make you slide up and down each other is pretty sensual stuff. Adding a few whispers of your desires makes this a good prelude to sexual intercourse. Direct, clear communication is also a come-on. Just murmur, "I want you."

91. Can massage serve as a prelude to sex?

There is nothing sexier than repeated gentle touching and stroking. Dr. Reinisch suggests that if massage is new to you, start on your mate's back, slowly move to stroke his arms, legs, and buttocks, and then, ever so tenderly, suggest that he turn over and begin to massage his front. If your partner doesn't communicate verbally about what feels good, try to judge by the little grunts and moans emitted when you've massaged a certain place or in a way that feels particularly good. Return to those spots frequently. If erection is a problem, gently massage around your partner's genitals before beginning your stroking technique on the penis itself. This same procedure ending with stroking the female genitalia works as a come-on for women as well.

92. Do sexy books turn most people on?

Many of the women I interviewed prefer a romantic novel to a romantic, erotic, or how-to video. They claim that, in a sense, less is more, meaning that suggestive prose carefully woven into the storyline allows them to invent their own imagery, endowing the characters with some of the characteristics and natures that they themselves find more enticing. The enormous sales of romance novels prove this point. As Casey told the group, "When he throws her on the bed, ripping her bodice, raising her skirt, and pounding his member into her quivering moist treasure box, . . . she could be me, because I have no finite picture of her before me."

93. *Do certain items of clothing send sexy signals?*

There is no consensus concerning sexy clothes, except for the informal survey I took, which revealed that suggestive is deemed sexier than blatant. For some partners, covering up with clothing presents more of a challenge and demands more of a conquest, which they like. In contrast, Jessica's lover says, "No nightgown, no perfume, just naked bodies." Other men and women report that they like their partners to start out scantily clothed, but with enough on to veil the treasures and to pique their sense of mystery and adventure. One man, an ardent lover in his mid-sixties, prefers his wife to go to bed in her old college-style ankle-length flannel nightgown with the high ruffled neck and the long sleeves, ruffled at the wrist. One person's sexy siren is another person's slut. Here again, this is a good subject for conversation with your mate. Try to find out what kind of clothing your partner finds sexually stimulating and if the shoe—or any other item of clothing—fits, wear it!

94. Why does my interest in sex return somewhat when we're on vacation and disappear again at home?

That's why they call it a vacation! Actually, in a long-term relationship we permit comfort to curtail creativity in our lovemaking. Routine and usual aren't all that exciting. As Dr. June Reinisch explains, "Even caviar every day is going to become routine." We have to work at keeping our sexuality stimulated. We have to break in a new routine now and then. New places, new positions, new times of day all help to keep the usual unusual. When you are at home the business and problems of your daily lives can crowd out your sex life. You may figure that you're busy today and there's always tomorrow to "do it." Sometimes, tomorrow never comes and neither do you. If everything is working well for you both on vacation, then you know that your problems are not hormonal, not physical, and maybe not even slightly psychological, but rather environmental. So make time and space for each other at home. Try to tempt and tease each other. One of you take the Sunday paper and coffee back to bed, summon your mate, lock the doors, and begin to stroke the other's back, limbs, and front with warmed almond oil. In no time, it will seem as if you're on vacation!

"You sense something is missing. The electric currents of passion that used to erupt when you passed one another in the hallway or the meltdown you felt when your hands touched as you exchanged notes are no longer there. You have the feeling that your furniture communicates more than you do."

—Erma Bombeck
*A Marriage Made in Heaven,
or Too Tired for an Affair*
HarperCollins, 1993

Questions for You

1. Are you comfortable enough with yourself to initiate sexual activity with your partner?

2. Where do you rank good sex on your list of ingredients for a happy life?

3. Have you ever tried to send sex signals about fooling around and getting ready for sex?

4. Have you ever given your partner a full body massage or have you ever gotten one?

5. Have you ever read erotic passages to your partner?

CHAPTER 11

How Do I Gain Sexual Energy Through Exercise?

❧

CASEY SAID THAT SHE AND her husband worked out so frequently that when they hit the sack, they fell asleep. "But sex was great when we had it," she confessed. Sometimes sex gets that way. It's more relaxed. The sex drive doesn't gnaw at you the way it did when you were younger and your hormones were racing around madly. There are no sexual dictums, except "use it or lose it." Frequency is not a subject for a locker room discussion; it's a joint decision, spoken or unspoken. For some of us, it's ideal that way.

Others, like me, every once in a while, have an *Elvira Madigan* attack. Do you remember that movie about romance and star-crossed lovers? When that happens I yearn to escape to our own private island and ride through sunny fields of flowers to the strains of Mozart's Piano Concerto in C Major, Number 21. When the longing gets too great and the time to fulfill it doesn't exist, I have to remind myself that ultimately Elvira Madigan and her lover died in self-imposed isolation—which proves, I suppose, that too much of a good thing is not a good idea. So I go and work out in the gym.

Somewhere between exercise instead of sex and exercise to forget about unrequited romantic longings lie the sexual virtues and verities of good long-term relationships and the caution we must bring to relationships, especially new ones, in a disease-ridden society. Exercise can help!

There are three types of exercise that midlife men and women require. We need to stretch for flexibility, perform aerobics to strengthen our hearts and lungs, and do weight-bearing exercise and perhaps even resistance training to maintain our muscle and bone mass. We also need to check with our physicians before we begin any *new* exercise program. A good exercise program might begin with a ten-minute warm-up involving gentle head-to-toe stretching, which lengthens our muscles, warms them, and gets them ready to work. Swimming is terrific for flexibility. Then try twenty to thirty minutes of aerobic activity, such as walking outside or on a treadmill, stair-climbing, or low-impact aerobics to get your heart to its target rate.

(To find your target heart rate, subtract your age from 220—then calculate 60 to 75 percent of that number to learn your target heart rate.) Finish with another ten minutes of stretching and you've had a great workout. On alternate days, add light weight-lifting preceded and followed by ten minutes of stretching and you have an excellent exercise program. The newest exercise theory is that we can gain the benefits of exercise in even shorter increments of time. So, if you don't have an hour to spare, divide your exercise into two, three, or four shorter segments. Take a day off every three or four days to rest your body, then begin again. What does exercise have to do with midlife sex, love, and intimacy? Lots.

Exercise is empowering. Control is empowering. Taking care of yourself is empowering, and the endorphins produced by exercise can help. They are the "happy" hormones that circulate through our systems in abundance when we exercise. Have you heard of the runner's high? It is caused by an increase in endorphin hormones. That speeded-up super sense of well-being can make your instinct for sexual gratification so strong that it's almost palpable.

Then there's the issue of wanting to share how good you feel and how good you look with a loved one or someone you'd like to make love with. Why not? Madonna isn't the only sex symbol. For some, she's not even a very good one! You can celebrate your own sexuality. Find your own private island.

At a spa retreat in Ohio, a group of women came to hear my lecture about menopause and osteoporosis, but it didn't take long for the question-and-answer period that followed to turn to the subject of sex. We had all been together for several days, exercising together, eating together, and sharing our war stories, so, huddled in sweat suits after a minimalist dinner, it was no surprise that we felt close enough to talk about sex, a subject that is usually and unfortunately still taboo in most social settings. A spa is somehow different.

We were quite a group, ranging in age from thirty-five to well-cared-for septuagenarians. Francie was thrice-married, blond, svelte, and around seventy. She blushed and giggled frequently and chided us hesitatingly and gently, saying, "We're the older generation here and we did not discuss sex as freely as the younger generation, don't you think?"

Polly, one of the aerobic leaders, about thirty-five and lean and mean, replied, "Well, maybe that's true. But we're very funny when it comes to talking about sex, too, yet when we do talk we learn more from other women than from anyone else. We even hesitate to talk about sex with a friend."

Another round of Perrier with lemon and we got into the discussion. Everyone wanted to know if it's true that you "use it or lose it." And what exactly do you lose? Do you lose the desire or just the capability, just your partner's ability, or what?

Sarah, a well-preserved seventy at least, blurted out, "Most men my age lose it! They're not capable anymore. They just can't maintain an erection, and if they don't resort to oral sex, they're in trouble."

"I disagree," came a chorus.

"If the man is healthy, he's in better shape sexually."

"Let me put it this way: I don't have any problems," said the zaftig, smirking Sylvia. "Maybe my husband isn't average."

Sarah made it quite clear that when she was younger, her mate made all the moves; now it's up to her. If she doesn't feel up to par or doesn't like her body, she can't take the aggressor role. "So I exercise and I eat less and I make the moves."

"I'm going home right now and have more sex. I don't want to lose it!" shouted Polly.

"Be ready, I'm coming home tomorrow—early," said Sylvia, feigning a phone call.

"I'm just going to crawl under the chair," said Francie, her face matching her hot-pink sweats.

There we sat, an unlikely group, driven together by our desire to feel better and look better through adopting healthier lifestyles and working out the greater part of every day during our time at the spa. We had walked, run, stepped, lifted, jumped, boxed, danced, done yoga and Tai Chi, all in the name of fitness.

We all had different reasons for this wonderful week of exercise excess, but basically they boiled down to feeling better and to looking better—sometimes for ourselves, but often for our significant other and in the mirror reflection of our world.

95. *Can exercise enhance my desire for sex?*

You bet it can. The endorphins produced by exercise provide reserve energy and underpin desire. Exercise also produces that "look good, feel good" state of mind that makes us want to shed our clothes and show off our bodies, proud of our handiwork. There is the flexibility attained from stretching and yoga that gets rid of our aches and pains by working our muscles and lubricating our joints. Exercise may be the very elixir of life and happiness. However, one caveat here: If your lack of sexual desire is born of a lack of testosterone or a psychological problem that you haven't dealt with, you should continue to exercise, but also check out the other situations with a professional. A selection of resources for finding a good gynecologist and a sex therapist or counselor appears in Appendix D.

96. *I'm not as "tight" as I once was. What exercises can help me?*

The Kegel exercises are the simplest, the most silent and secretive, and can be the most seductive. Named for Dr. Arnold Kegel, the California physician who first described them, they are good for both women and men. Yoga practice has long demonstrated their benefit for women and men.

97. *What are the Kegel exercises?*

Basically, the Kegels are contraction exercises in which you tighten the muscles in the pelvic area, the muscles of the bladder among them. The best way to locate the muscles that you want to work on is to try to interrupt the flow of urine. It's exactly those muscles that you want to grab, tighten, and hold for a count of ten. Release. Groups of ten to twelve of these exercises done five or six times a day can be very helpful in retaining a more youthful tone to the pelvic muscles. When women perform Kegels during intercourse, the effect can be very pleasurable to both the woman and the man.

98. *Exactly how do I perform Kegels?*

There are actually two kinds of Kegels. There is a slow version and a fast one. In the slow version, pull in the pelvic muscles hard and tight, hold for a count of ten, relax and repeat. In the fast Kegel, you can contract and release quickly. Try both and see which form works best for you, or alternate them as I do. There is now on the market a biofeedback computer distributed by InCare Medical Products to help a woman know whether she is performing her Kegel exercises correctly and, if not, how to correct them to regain lost vaginal tone. The instrument is composed of a small computer and a tampon-size miniprobe for vaginal insertion. It can also perform your Kegels for you by emitting electrical pulses that cause involuntary contractions—in other words, automatic Kegels—for women who have trouble doing them. There are other new products on the market as well for helping you do Kegel exercises. Ask your physician what she or he can recommend for you if you need help.

99. *Should I try to do the Kegels during intercourse?*

Women have reported a distinct pleasurable sensation from doing the Kegels during intercourse. Some like the fast version; others the slow. Men also report pleasure from feeling the vagina tighten and relax around the penis, providing a throbbing sensation which they report as deeply satisfying and often helping to maintain their erection, make a slightly flaccid penis more rigid, or bring on ejaculation more quickly (sometimes too quickly, so watch out!).

100. *Can a fit body make me more desirous of sex?*

Often we feel more seductive and more sensuous when we feel and look fit and are thus able to give and receive more pleasure. This is not true for all of us. Many women are lucky, having deep wells of desire that operate irrespective of their perceived fitness. But as the *Mademoiselle* survey (discussed in the answer to Question 24) demonstrated, many women of all ages feel sexier when they feel fit.

101. *I feel much more sluggish now than I ever have. I'm too tired for sex. What exercises will pick me up?*

Studies have shown that when we're tired, we are better off doing some form of exercise rather than resting. If fatigue and sluggishness are new for you, check with your physician first to make sure that no physiological problems are causing your fatigue and discuss with her or him what kind of exercise you should begin with once you've received a clean bill of health. A lack of reserve energy also can emanate from psychological problems, so ponder that possibility as well. Once your good health is confirmed, you may wish to discuss testosterone replacement, because reproductive endocrinologist Ted Quigley reports significant leaps in energy in women taking small amounts of that male sex hormone. There is no doubt that the better shape you're in, the better sex can be.

102. What other positions can help my partner and me to enjoy sex? He is rather overweight and I have osteoporosis.

According to the experts with whom I have discussed this subject, it is important that you be in a position in which you have a great deal of control so that no surprising or sudden moves can harm your fragile bones. This kind of control often comes from your being on top and astride your mate so that the sexual pulsing can be done by you. That is also a pleasure position for many women, enabling them to control the stroking and to help bring themselves to orgasm at a pace they find satisfying. A side-to-side, face-to-face position may also be good for you, as can "spoons": his front to your back. I suggest that you begin to try different positions to learn the comfort and safety of each. Taking new positions on the subject of sex is a good idea, anyway, providing challenge and excitement and requiring good communication with your partner. If explicit drawings do not turn you off, take a look at *The New Joy of Sex* by Dr. Alex Comfort for some variations.

103. Is there a value to experimenting with activities to turn us on, or are we too old?

Of course you should experiment. You're never too old for good sex. The only problem we sometimes have in long-term relationships is sexual boredom. Part of what makes an affair exciting is its inherent danger, mystery, and novelty. These are the kinds of qualities you need to bring into your own sex life. Throughout this book on pages 83, 175, 176. I have made suggestions for films, videotapes, and books that may help you. A young woman, Deborah Shames, has recently produced a video called *Cabin Fever,* an explicit erotic production in the form of a story, which Dr. Reinisch says is what most women prefer. Don't give up your sex life, recharge it!

"One of the simplest ways to prevent entropy is to give the body something to do."

—Deepak Chopra, M.D.
Ageless Body, Timeless Mind
Harmony Books, 1993

Questions for You

1. Do you do Kegel exercises regularly?

2. Do you perform Kegels during sexual intercourse?

3. Do you exercise regularly, performing flexibility, aerobic, and weight-bearing exercises?

4. Is your partner in good physical shape?

5. Have you ever experimented with new approaches, new positions, or with utilizing new sources of erotica to spice up your sex life?

CHAPTER 12

What Is
a Good Sex
Diet?

THE WOMEN IN THE FOCUS GROUPS, at the spa, in the various surveys, and from individual and couple interviews all have the same lament: "If only I were thinner/ weighed less/ had bigger boobs/ smoother skin/ a firmer bottom/ sleeker thighs/ a flatter belly/ more luxuriant hair, my life would be better/ happier/ sexier."

What's preventing us from being our personal best is only our personal selves. Either from not understanding that plump can be beautiful (think of Rubens's women) or that many of us cannot achieve our sought-after ideal because we are not genetically capable of staying ultra-thin—even if we force ourselves to get there—any more than we can make ourselves taller or shorter, we make ourselves miserable and unsexy instead of accentuating our positives.

Thankfully, after years of being bombarded with the super-thin and the super-young models, this unattainable goal is about to change. Witness *The New York Times* headline (January 24, 1994): "AS CUSTOMERS AGE, MARKETERS DISCOVER NEW NOTION OF BEAUTY." Forty-four-year-old Ken Dychtwald, Ph.D. a gerontologist from Emeryville, California, who advises corporate clients about marketing to midlife and senior adults through his Age Wave company, is quoted in the article: "The 50-plus generation is growing by 12 million people in this decade alone," Dychtwald said. "And they are recession proof. In this decade alone they are going to have over 300 billion dollars in spending power."

Companies like Nike and Estée Lauder are listening. They are also aware of the 1990 Census Bureau statistics showing that there are almost sixteen million women ages forty to forty-nine in the United States—36 percent more than in 1980. So former top model Lauren Hutton was recycled at the age of fifty and she looks out at us from magazine covers and ads and billboards, gap-toothed and gorgeous, and while we still don't look like her, we feel more comfortable with her now. We must rethink ourselves, understanding that we don't need to look like her or anyone else to be sexy or to be happy.

We have finally arrived at the age when we can act instead of react. We can choose instead of being chosen. We can be who we are, look the way we do, and be interesting, exciting, and desirable. We are not invisible; we are no longer waiting, mannequinlike, for anyone to look for or at us. We are animated; we are looking at you, looking around, and making choices. I have a friend who always says that any woman who wants to marry or remarry can and will, if she decides to take an assertive role in locating a mate. Those women who wait, waiflike, to be selected often aren't. At midlife, men, too, have their own vast array of insecurities and many prefer a woman's making the first move to risking their own egos all the time.

What does this have to do with diet? Diet is an important consideration. I'm talking about diet, not dieting. A good healthful diet can do wonders for your hair, skin, nails, thighs, belly, waistline, and bottom. A nutritious diet of low-fat, high-fiber, calcium-rich foods plus eight eight-ounce glasses of water a day can do all that and more. Myths abound when it comes to sexual energy from foods, and eminent sexologist Dr. June Reinisch assures me that they remain myths. Yet there are some herbal aphrodisiacs that may tone or stimulate our sexual organs. *Vitex,* or chasteberry, is the herb most recommended by some alternative medicine practitioners for its hormone-balancing qualities. It is said to act by stimulating and normalizing the pituitary gland. You may also wish to review the discussion of damiana, red clover, and vanilla described on page 173 as well.

104. Will eating raw oysters make me feel sexier?

No, but they can make you sick. For a long time we were told only to eat raw oysters in months that contain the letter R so April was okay, but not May. Today, we are cautioned against eating raw oysters at all because of the fear of contamination by other organisms in our polluted waters. So if you like oysters, eat them cooked. If you were only slurping them down raw because you believed they were imbued with aphrodisiac powers, forget them.

105. Do carbohydrates help to give sexual energy?

Carbohydrates are a good energy source and can help you overcome fatigue, enabling you to have energy for sex. An important caution, however: Before a sexual encounter, do not eat a big meal, which may make you feel sluggish and heavy when you would rather feel light and airy.

106. *Are cocktails a good solution for getting rid of my midlife inhibitions about sex?*

Although a small amount of alcohol can loosen up some individuals, alcohol can be a depressant for many and it can delay orgasm in women and reduce potency in men. According to a bulletin from the Department of Health and Human Services, "alcohol is probably the most widespread cause of sexual problems." In addition to damaging your liver and interfering with a host of other bodily functions, large amounts of alcohol can exacerbate PMS and menopause symptoms, weaken your bones, and, in men, can wreak havoc with their ability to attain or sustain an erection. I would try to work out inhibitions through counseling or therapy rather than masking them with alcohol or any other substances. I admit that a glass of wine at the end of the work day can be a healthful and relaxing reward, but I would not use it to relieve sexual inhibitions, especially because in the current scary sexual environment it's better to be thinking clearly as part of practicing safer sex.

107. *If I try to starve to stay thin, I feel nervous. If I eat I feel too fat to enjoy sex. What's a happy medium?*

Obviously, you are too focused on how you look to discover how you feel. Good sex is not a matter of how thin or how fat you are, but rather how much sexual pleasure and intimacy you are able to give and to receive. I would suggest that you are letting worries about your weight affect other facets of your life and that you must come to grips with your mirror image. If you recall the *Mademoiselle* magazine survey in Chapter 4, you will note that even very young women, ages eighteen to thirty, believe that their sex lives would improve if they weighed less, so this is not only a midlife matter. Studies show that not everyone's body is genetically programmed to be as thin as we might like and that no matter how hard we work to stay ultra-thin, our own genetic set point works even harder to reset itself. Pick a comfortable weight for yourself, try to stay there, and get on with your sex life. If this continues to be a problem, seek help.

108. My mate says that he likes me just as I am. Shouldn't he be more involved in keeping me looking and feeling sexy?

Lucky lady! Don't complain about a mate who likes you as you are; he is undoubtedly content with you. No, I don't think it is our partner's job to monitor our appearance, especially our weight. It's *our* job! Nobody ever lost weight for anyone else. It cannot be done. We lose weight for ourselves.

109. What usually comes first, the weight problem or the sex problem?

Often it is the psychological problem that makes weight or sex a concern. Women tell me that after menopause they have gained between ten and forty pounds or more. That is probably in part a metabolic problem (our metabolism slows down from about age thirty-five on at the rate of ½ to 1 percent per year), and we need to eat more nutritiously—low-fat, high-fiber, calcium-rich food—and exercise more. If the weight gain is minimal, it may be a hormone-related problem caused by water retention or it can be depression that is causing you to accept food for love. Try to get help in sorting out your problems. You may wish to start with your own physician. Write down your questions and concerns so that you can have a productive appointment, get your questions answered, and start to rebuild your self-image and to restart your sexual engine.

110. When I lose weight, I feel nervous, as if my protective wrapper is gone. Why is that and what can I do about it?

A hypertension and obesity specialist with whom I worked at Mt. Sinai Medical Center in Cleveland always referred to that as the seventh veil. It's as if we wrap ourselves in protective layers to keep us from looking as great as we might and, perhaps, to protect ourselves from living out our fantasies. He related this to me often when we discussed why people can't keep off that last ten pounds that they gain and lose literally hundreds of times throughout their lives. What you can do about it is seek help from a therapist.

111. My physician seems to indicate that I am at fault for my midlife weight gain. Why is that and why doesn't he help me instead of blaming me?

As discussed in the answer to Question 109, some water retention is possible for some women on hormone therapy. There is also the issue of metabolic slowdown which can catch up with us about the time of menopause, requiring us to eat better and exercise more. I must admit, however, that I do not believe scientific research has discovered all the reasons for this vexing problem. Some doctors say, "You gained weight because you eat too much." I don't think that's the full answer for many women. It's not that simple! Perhaps telling us "you don't eat the right kinds of foods" would help us more. Some recent studies do show greater weight gain in women on hormone replacement therapy that is not simply water-retention based. This is a knowledge gap and until medical research delivers some better answers, I believe we have to do the best we can to keep our weight down, but not be dismayed if we gain a few pounds that we can't shake.

112. *Is there a difference in the kind of water retention I experienced when I was premenstrual and the kind of bloating I am suffering with now at midlife?*

Whether or not you took birth control pills when you were premenopausal and if you are now on combined estrogen and progestin therapy (HRT) or estrogen replacement therapy (ERT), the source of the water retention can be exactly the same: either caused by the cyclic rise in estrogen in your system or by your hormone regimen. Some physicians tell us that we can expect a hormonally induced weight gain of four to eight pounds, caused primarily by water retention. Surprisingly, though, it is by drinking water that you can fight water retention and bloating naturally. Water is the best diuretic. Eight eight-ounce glasses of water each day will help you in so many ways, ridding the body of extra fluids and of waste while helping you to metabolize stored fat and maintain good muscle tone. Vitamin B_6 in small amounts can also help rid the body of excess fluids. The following foods also have natural diuretic action: alfalfa, asparagus, celery, dandelion greens, and carrots.

113. Does seafood make you sexy?

As with oysters, discussed in Question 104, the answer is no. But it can make you thirsty, thereby adding to your fluid retention problem. This kind of salt-induced thirst makes the water you drink stay with you longer, causing bloating for a while. When I eat seafood for dinner, I invariably wake up with "sausage fingers" because I am so water-filled.

114. Is there a vitamin supplement or homeopathic remedy that can help increase my sex drive?

Some studies suggest that a lack of zinc, one of the trace minerals, in the diet can cause a lack of lubrication in women and impotence in men. According to Deborah Grossman, a registered nurse whose primary interest is in homeopathy, there is no homeopathic remedy simply for enhancement of the sex drive. She states that usually there is some underlying factor that may be diminishing the sex drive, and when that is uncovered and a remedy is taken, your sex drive will improve.

115. Is there any category of foods that increase libido?

I hear this question repeatedly, be it about oysters, seafood, alcohol, and even drugs. The answer remains that a healthful diet is all that I can recommend for libido. Foods that are too fatty or carbohydrate-loaded and weigh you down can make you too sluggish for sex. Foods that cause gas are also to be avoided before lovemaking, as are those that upset your stomach in other ways. There is no food that you can eat to drive your libido, but high-fat diets can have negative sexual consequences. There is some research under way (not yet published) that relates high cholesterol to impotence, possibly caused by impaired blood vessels, as well as some suspicion that the lack of lubrication in some women may be caused by cholesterol blockages in blood vessels.

116. *Are there any herbs that I can take to enhance my sexuality?*

The Chinese herb schizandra is reported to enhance sexual performance. Some say that schizandra can help men with erection difficulties and that chasteberry (*Vitex*) can help women. There are a number of herbal remedies which may help, but these require individual treatment. A number of men and women have written to me to praise acupuncture for lifting their levels of sexual desire. Other women write to me of success with ginseng, dong quai, black cohosh, valerian, and evening primrose oil, which by alleviating their menopausal symptoms have helped to make them feel better and more in the mood for sex. Damiana is believed to be a sexual stimulant for both men and women, although that has not been scientifically proven. Folk medicine tells us that asparagus and artichoke hearts increase feelings of love and are aphrodisiacs for both sexes. If your male partner has an impotence problem, you may wish to discuss with your doctor the possibility of treatment using the bark of the yohimbe tree. Another good source for help would be a homeopathic specialist who could work out an individual remedy for your problems. There is a list of organizations that can help you find a practitioner in your area in Appendix D.

"But food has no power other than what we give it. Food is just food, nothing more or less."

—Dean Ornish, M.D.
Eat More, Weigh Less
HarperCollins, 1993

Questions for You

1. Are you satisfied with your body image?

2. Can you identify what is keeping you from being your personal best?

3. At midlife, do you feel more self-assured, more able to choose what is important to you and to act upon it?

4. Do you eat nutritious meals whenever possible and drink at least eight eight-ounce glasses of water each day?

5. Have you ever looked into using any herbal remedies for sexuality enhancement?

CHAPTER 13

How Do I Fulfill
My Sexual Needs
When I'm Flying Solo?

IN 1993, IN HER much-read and beloved column, which runs in more than 1200 newspapers across the United States, Ann Landers answered a question and turned the concept of masturbation around 180 degrees. She responded in simple terms to a woman's question and was able to do what no one else could achieve—she made masturbation respectable in a way that sexologists, psychiatrists, psychologists, and other professionals have been trying to do for years.

In that much-praised (sometimes criticized) column, Landers wrote that the practice of self-gratification should be considered a safe, realistic sexual alternative for everyone from the teenager to the elderly.

Everyone, including the characters on *Seinfeld* and *Roseanne,* have tried to uncover the subject of masturbation recently. Yet it still seems that people are more comfortable talking about almost anything else. Is it the moral issue or strong religious rejection that continue to make this M-word taboo?

This may be one of those issues that is considered okay as long as we don't discuss it, particularly not in polite company, and although individuals indicate interest in the topic on my questionnaires, they know the questionnaires are anonymous.

Sex educators often tell us that masturbation can release sexual tension, teach us about our own bodies, help us find our erogenous zones, and give us sexual pleasure. When you have no partner, or want no partner, sexual self-gratification is a legitimate route to take. So masturbation is okay. It's a natural part of life and a safe alternative to AIDS, STDs, and unwanted pregnancy.

The preachy "no-no's" that remain are seated in religious bodies where twin beliefs offer the major opposition to masturbation. One belief is that a primary reason for intercourse is procreation and the other is that sexuality is a gift to be shared only with one's spouse. That was then; this is now. We've got to begin to talk seriously about our bodies, about sexual pleasure, and about masturbation.

The *Janus Report on Sexual Behavior* showed that 55

percent of men and 38 percent of women masturbate regularly. Two-thirds of the individuals surveyed viewed masturbation as a natural part of life. Only 6 percent of the married men and 12 percent of the married women said that they had never masturbated. In *Love and Sex After 60,* Dr. Robert Butler, chairman of the Department of Geriatric Medicine at Manhattan's Mount Sinai School of Medicine, and Myrna I. Lewis, M.S.W., state: "Self-stimulation, or masturbation, is a common and healthy practice that usually begins in childhood. . . . Self-stimulation provides a sexual outlet for people—unmarried, widowed, or divorced—who do not have partners, as well as for husbands or wives whose partners are ill or away. . . . Masturbation can continue until very late in life."

The support for masturbation is out there. In the 1990 *Merck Manual,* it was reported that 80 percent of females and 97 percent of males have masturbated at some time in their lives. In *Sex Over Forty,* Dr. Saul H. Rosenthal notes, "Masturbation is a good way of keeping sexual function intact during the time when a partner is unavailable. Some couples additionally include masturbation as an occasional part of their lovemaking together." He writes that a fairly recent study reported that one-half of the women and two-thirds of the men surveyed masturbate at various times.

The *Kinsey Report* published in the 1950s reported that of the literally thousands of persons interviewed in the previous two decades, 40 percent of the women and 94 percent of the men had masturbated to orgasm. So although no one survey agrees exactly with another, it is evident that a large number of women and men masturbate. Even though they don't want to talk about it, they *do* want to have sexual release. In fact, according to the National Institute of Aging publication *Age Page:* "Sexuality in Later Life," "most older people want and are able to lead an active satisfying sex life." Often this may translate into solo sex for some women and men when a partner is not available or not sought. Although response time may have become slower, obviously masturbation is a very satisfying form of sexual expression.

117. *Is masturbation harmful?*

In *The Kinsey Institute New Report on Sex* authored by June M. Reinisch, Ph.D., with Ruth Beasley, M.L.S., Dr. Reinisch writes, "The most important things to know about masturbation are that the vast majority of people do it and that, unless a person uses an extraordinarily rough or violent technique, masturbation does not cause any kind of physical harm." Dr. Reinisch's answer indicates that there is no harm in masturbation unless it is caused by the nature of the technique. Most health professionals agree. Some theologians, however, express a negative view, noting that early masturbation can turn a person inward; that it can cause them to associate sex with pleasure-taking instead of pleasure-giving, obliterating the concept of sex as a loving, selfless act; and that masturbation can become an addiction. If you are asking about whether masturbation is harmful to your health, the answer is a resounding *no*. If your question regards your soul, that is another matter, which you will have to work out with clergy or counselor.

118. How often should I masturbate in order to keep my sexual organs in good shape?

As often as it pleases you and helps you to feel good. It's just like having sex, only it's solo. Masturbation is a healthy pursuit. The frequency of masturbation varies greatly; some people increase or decrease the frequency depending on life circumstances, and others stay at the same rate, according to Dr. Reinisch. Even Sigmund Freud changed his view on masturbation when, in 1925 at the age of sixty-nine, he recanted his earlier teaching that masturbation was the cause of what he called "the actual neurosis."

119. *What kinds of vibrators work best?*

Interestingly, most vibrators are advertised for massage rather than for sexual stimulation, so take your time when you shop to find the type that suits your purposes best. There are phallic-shaped vibrators that can be inserted into the vagina, so if that brings you pleasure you will want that shape. However, if you use the vibrator in the genital area outside the vagina—as do most women—another type may be more satisfactory. A number of hand-held models come with three or four different vibrating heads, giving you the opportunity to try various types to see what suits you the best. It is also a good idea to get one with a couple of speed settings so that you can vary the intensity as you wish.

120. *Where can I buy a vibrator and get some information on how to use it?*

Vibrators are usually carried in drugstores, in some department stores, and are available through mail order catalogues. If they do carry instructions, they will probably not be for sexual stimulation. I suggest that you try to find out what stimulates you best by starting with the slowest vibration speed and some lubrication, and moving gently around the genital region, exploring each tender area for pleasurable sensations. Most women report that vibrating the clitoris brings them the greatest arousal and carries them to orgasm.

121. *What are some reliable and helpful vibrators?*

Some brands of vibrators that are reported to work well include the Hitachi Magic Wand, Hitachi Magic Touch plus Massager, the Sunbeam Coil, and the Conair Family Fitness Bodytherm Wand massager. There are many other brands as well.

122. *Is there a need to maintain some kind of sexual self-stimulation for health reasons?*

The vagina changes in a number of important ways as we age, especially if we do not use it. It can tend to become dryer and shorter. The changes in lubrication, flexibility, and shape can be traced directly to lowered levels of estrogen. These changes can be increasingly problematic as we age and difficult to reverse should we then wish to resume sex with a partner later in life. Older men often notice that it takes somewhat longer to obtain an erection and that it may not be as firm or as large, or there may be a shorter time of sensation of impending ejaculation and a longer span of time between erections. For both men and women there are advantages to maintaining some sexual activity, whether via masturbation or with a partner.

123. My sex drive is intact, but I don't have a partner any longer. Where do you suggest that I find someone?

On page 90, I listed many places where you can go to seek companionship. These are good choices, if they are places that you are interested in, enabling you to meet someone with mutual interests. Family, friends, and coworkers remain a good source for meeting people. There are a number of dating services and personal columns in reputable magazines and newspapers that work well, too. Just make sure that you check the references of the services, the columns, and any callers that you may hear from as a result.

124. After a very long, very bad marriage I am finally single again. I am trying to connect with a partner for sex and companionship only. I will never marry again. How do I check out a prospective partner for HIV or any other sexually transmitted disease?

I asked several doctors whether a certificate demonstrating a clean bill of health was a good and protective idea. They all said that it was good for the three or four months before the test was done, not later because of the gestation period of the HIV virus. In the interim between the test and when you have intercourse with the partner, there may have been other partners and other sources of HIV or STDs. Obviously, it's a good idea to know the person pretty well before considering a sexual liaison. But even that is no guarantee. Sexologist Dr. June Reinisch suggests perhaps being tested together when you are sure you are committing to an exclusive relationship and are planning to use condoms anyway. For the safest sex, she suggests using a good spermicide inside the condom on the male and having the female use a diaphragm with spermicide as well. Nonoxyl 9 is a good choice. Or, for good sex, consider mutual masturbation, which may represent the ultimate intimacy and the safest sex.

> "We're brother and sister. Don't knock it. It has its own strange allure. And it lasts longer than sex."
>
> —Erica Jong
> *Any Woman's Blues*
> HarperCollins, 1990

Questions for You

1. Have you ever masturbated?

2. Have you and a partner ever practiced mutual masturbation?

3. Have you ever used a vibrator to reach orgasm?

4. If you are not in an exclusive long-term relationship, do you discuss HIV, AIDS, and STDs and protect yourself against them?

5. Do you insist that your partner use a condom?

CHAPTER 14

What Are Good Midlife Sexual Ethics and Politics?

GOD SAVE US from being inappropriate. That was the cry of my generation. The fifties. We probably gave birth to the wild and woolly sixties in order to save the world from boring propriety. Then along came diseases to spoil all the fun. First we were frightened to learn that herpes is forever; then we learned that AIDS meant death. Now we're back to the boring fifties. Or are we?

In my discussion groups, three of the women who were widowed or divorced admitted to picking up men in bars and using no protection. Had the sense of midlife immortality patterned itself after the young? Or didn't they care just then what happened to them?

Mirabella magazine did us a service with a reader survey entitled "How's Your Health," cosponsored by the Center for Women Policy Studies, to which seven thousand well-off readers responded. Some interesting facts emerged from these women eighteen to sixty years of age, nearly half of them married, and nearly all well educated and employed in professional or managerial positions.

Most women (87 percent) were non-smokers; 39 percent considered themselves overweight; more than half drank half of the suggested amount of water each day (four glasses, 50.8 percent), craved chocolate and ice cream, and exercised three times a week (60 percent, the favored activity being walking outdoors); almost half over the age of fifty-five were on hormone therapy (the fact that 31.2 percent of the respondents aged forty-five to fifty-four are also on hormone therapy was among the many statistics that emerged). Now let's get to the sex part.

The married respondents say they are not worried about AIDS (66.9 percent), although some admit to having had more than one partner; of the unmarried respondents, only 35.7 percent always use condoms to protect themselves against AIDS, yet many insist on knowing their partners' sexual history. Are we playing roulette, or what?

Eminent physiologist Dr. Estelle Ramey makes no bones about the sexual dangers inherent in sex outside

of a long-term exclusive relationship. The same senti-
ment is echoed by every single doctor I interviewed,
regardless of discipline. We must take the danger seriously. Is this the time of "The Silent Plague?" Why
would we voluntarily expose ourselves to diseases that
can kill us?

More than six million women in the United States
contract a sexually transmitted disease each year. Sadly,
half of that number are teenagers. The diseases are
rampant: chlamydia, herpes, gonorrhea, pelvic inflam-
matory disease, syphilis, and the HIV virus leading to
AIDS. In some cities, AIDS is the leading cause of
death for women aged fifteen to forty-nine. In 1990 the
largest increase in AIDS cases was among women who
are drug abusers, and heterosexual sex became the
leading means of transmission. The impact of STDs
upon women is greater for two reasons, according to
Patricia Donovan, author of *Testing Positive,* a publication of the Alan Guttmacher Institute. The first is,
quite simply, because women can receive transmission
of the diseases more easily and the second is that these
diseases, some of which may be asymptomatic, are
more difficult to diagnose in women than in men, so
they can progress further and do more damage before
they are diagnosed.

Dr. Ramey explains that as women age the quality

of their lubrication changes, frequently causing fissures or cracks in the lining of the vagina. These are good hiding places that enable disease to thrive. We must take seriously the challenge that the HIV and STDs environment has thrust upon us and our children. We must be educated about safer sex and we must practice it. Research findings of a survey conducted by the Sex Information and Education Council of the United States show that just 10 percent of young Americans receive adequate sex education and that families in the U.S. rank sexual difficulties as their fourth most serious problem, following finances, domestic violence, and their responses to societal upheaval.

125. If I hear "use it or lose it" one more time, I'll go nuts. I am trying to communicate my sexual needs to the man I am now seeing. How explicit should I be?

Be completely honest and forthright. According to Candace B. Risen, L.I.S.W., co-director of the Center for Marital and Sexual Health in Cleveland and assistant clinical professor of social work in psychiatry at Case Western Reserve University, "We have to ask for what we want." There is nothing wrong with establishing clear communications about your sexual needs, wants, and desires. Dr. Reinisch often calls communication the best lubricant.

126. Why does society think of senior adults as non-sexual?

The word has not circulated even yet that sexuality is a lifelong attribute unless you turn it off or it becomes impaired by illness. The early work in this field comes from many sources, yet it has not filtered down to the masses, even in the retirement communities or nursing homes. I interviewed a friend in a lovely retirement village about a year ago. She is "seeing a man" who lives across the hall. She has never been more content, except for a problem with the staff: Each evening they go looking for her. She bemoans the fact that they don't understand that she and he are together and that they are having a perfectly wonderful time. Instead, the staff frequently interrupts them when they are watching television or "whatever." "You'd think they'd know better," she says.

127. I am too embarrassed to look in the library or in adult bookstores for sexually explicit materials that might turn me on, so how can I obtain information about them?

I'd like to suggest that you make an appointment with a sex counselor or therapist in your area for help with a list of materials that might work for you and to help you get over some of your embarrassment. Different kinds of information and presentation work for some individuals and not for others. Some women tell me that they are more comfortable with suggestive rather than explicit sexual materials.

Throughout this book, I have recommended movies, videotapes, and books. Perhaps you might try some of these suggestion and see whether they turn you on. Additional resources may be found in the Appendix.

128. Have we become too socially correct to find love at school or at work?

The number of sexual harassment complaints has sky-rocketed in the last few years as women and men try hard to figure out when or whether a flirt is too overt. Spawned by the Clarence Thomas and Anita Hill hearings, sensitivity to the issue of sexual harassment continues to rise. Watershed events such as this empower women, confuse or anger men, and bring a chill to executive boardrooms and workplace bathrooms and cafeterias everywhere. Books follow each other into the marketplace: Katie Roiphe writes of women who are making too much of date rape and Linda Fairstein tells of prosecuting sexual offenders. Now Michael Crichton's bestselling novel *Disclosure* reverses the issue and the woman becomes the harasser. Candace Risen, co-director of the center for Marital and Sexual Health, cautions us that women's views of men aren't very flattering. She reports that in her practice, which deals largely with men, men say how demeaned they are by our culture's view of men and what they believe is women's view of them. "It's not just women who can feel devalued, it's men, too. We all have to be careful, because there's a lot of male-bashing going on." Yet men think it is funny and unmanly for other men to be fearful of women's sexual aggressions. Women, on the other hand, are often just afraid for themselves and their jobs. Candace Risen explains that our best tool for handling this issue is clear and firm—not angry or provocative—communication. Men have long been used to doing and saying certain things that are inappropriate, depersonalizing, and degrading. If their attentions are unasked for and unwanted, then they have crossed the boundary of what is appropriate. We have to say so loud and clear. We have to talk before we act. Candace Risen describes women harassers as having a style that is more seductive. "Women are more manipulative and more verbal. Men are more grabby," she says. Yes, it is still possible to meet potential partners at school or at work, but it is important to be up front, respectful, and honest with each other so that nobody gets hurt or loses her or his job. It is important to remember that men are not the enemy and women are not hapless victims. We've got to learn to work together.

129. Is there any way that women can change from being objectified to being accepted for who they are?

I do not think the problem is so much that we are objectified, but rather that we objectify. Some women set impossible standards for themselves. They lie about their ages, yet they know in their heart of hearts that that does not make them younger. They suffer anorexia or bulimia because they have a psychological problem in accepting their own bodies. They need help. Some women smoke, drink, and take drugs in an effort to cope with their lives. We have got to learn to love ourselves, to take care of ourselves, to see and accept an accurate mirror image of ourselves, and to refuse to be abused physically, verbally, or emotionally.

130. My adult children worry about my purity and safety every time I go out on a date. How can I explain to them that sex is still very important to me without embarrassing them or me?

This most difficult of all conversations should be held as soon as possible. Let your children know that sexual desires and drives are lifelong normal factors in one's life. Tell them that you feel fortunate that you have not lost your lust for life or for sex. Remind them that sex is a healthful activity, that you practice it safely, that it offers a route to intimacy, and that besides, it's fun!

Throughout this book references are made to lifelong sex. Perhaps you could pick out some of the quotes from the experts and ask your children to read them in order to reassure themselves that your sexual desires are normal and appropriate. Keep the conversation clear and light and remember that they are only doing to you what all of us did to our unmarried children as they claimed their sexual freedom. It may be uncomfortable for your children to be aware of your sexual needs initially, but it seems worse for them to believe that it's okay to live without physical intimacy and love.

131. The condom has become the necessity of the nineties. Is there any playful way to make sure my partner puts one on and that there is no leakage?

The highest degree of protection we can have from HIV and other STDs is to make sure our partners use a condom. Putting on the condom can become part of the sex play. Ask him to let you put it on. Then in a carefree manner on an erect or semi-erect penis, place the condom around the glans and carefully roll it down the stalk of the penis. Make it an enjoyable process for you both. During sex play and intercourse, you can wrap your fingers around the base of the condom to assure there is no spilling when your partner ejaculates. If you treat the condom, in its many colors and flavors, as a part of the sex play instead of as a nuisance or bother, it can become part of the sex action instead of an interruption.

132. I live in a retirement community. You would think that all of the social workers here would understand that for some of us our need for sexual expression continues to the end. How can I get them to be respectful of senior sex, love, and intimacy?

I have asked that question in several retirement and nursing home settings, and when the staff answers my questions regarding senior sex, some seem to do it with a giggle. So I think you are right that many of these establishments do not take a respectful stance when it comes to later-life relationships. I hope that will change and that this book will help. In the meantime, feel sorry for those who do not comprehend and need to treat lightly what they are uncomfortable with. It is their problem, not yours.

133. Is it all right to suggest to my mate of fifty years that he get a prostitute to help him out sexually?

You are treading on dangerous ground in this disease-laden society. If illness is not your problem, I would sooner see you both get counseling in a marital or sexual therapy setting to see whether you can find a mutually agreeable way to solve your sexual disequilibrium. Several organizations are listed in Appendix D that can help you locate a good therapist or counselor in your area.

134. The only way I get turned on is when I cheat on my partner. Can extramarital sex be sanctioned somehow? Is it common?

The boredom of sex in a long-term relationship raises its head again. It occurs for some couples because there is no mystery, no novelty, and no danger in the encounters. Those are some of the factors that make an extramarital liaison exciting and satisfying. In the seventies and even the early eighties some couples had what was then referred to as "open marriages." That meant, I believe, that each partner could have other partners without damaging the relationship. Hmm. Maybe. Then along came STDs and AIDS and open marriages became truly dangerous, driving sexual fidelity home. Ideally, what we should all do is learn ways to make sex exciting in a long-term relationship by changing locations, positions, and whatever else you can think of. After all, if he always starts here and then moves to there, at which point you do this and he does that, it's not terribly adventuresome for either of you. So start by having sex in the living room after breakfast in bed, or meeting each other in a motel on the highway where you won't be seen, in the middle of the work day. Try anything, try everything to bring life back into your sex play. Of course, extramarital sex is common for both men and women, but not as common as it was before we had all these health considerations to contend with.

135. Is a lesbian relationship more liable to offer an understanding of the hormonal and bodily changes in the partners so that there is less pressure on looking young and more concern with providing sexual pleasure?

Every expert I've interviewed agrees that there can be more understanding of age-related changes in a lesbian relationship. Because women are alike in so many ways, it is easier to give understanding to one another. After all, women have been governed by their hormones since puberty, and if we didn't have bad PMS ourselves, we knew someone who did. That kind of understanding is the cornerstone of a good, long-term midlife relationship, and it is the idea of growing older and better together that helps shift the emphasis from struggling to stay young-looking to looking forward to the new freedoms and challenges that come with aging gracefully, enabling partners to come together in a new way and with renewed intimacy.

"All sex roles are up for redefinition, and it's not a bad thing either; loosening the stereotypical straitjackets on women may also free men."

—Nancy Friday
Women On Top
Simon & Schuster, 1991

Questions for You

1. Have you discussed your sexuality and any changes that have occurred with your physician?

2. Have you ever discussed with your partner making the condom part of your sex play?

3. Have you ever been a victim of sexual harassment?

4. Have you ever sexually harassed any of your coworkers?

5. Do you lie about your age?

CHAPTER 15

Why Don't Our Doctors Talk to Us About Our Sex Lives and Where Can I Go for Help?

I ONCE ASKED MY PHYSICIAN, "Why didn't you warn me of the side effects of this medication?" He replied pleasantly, "Because then you might have encountered them by suggestion." "Is this the placebo effect in reverse?" I questioned him further. "Not really," he said. "But if I listed all the possible side effects of a medication to all of my patients, I'd be here all day listing and then any symptom that came along could be blamed on the medication and the patient would discontinue its use. I think it's better to treat side effects as they occur." Yet a physician can often prescribe a drug with fewer sexual side effects if she or he realizes it is important to the patient. How many of us go about the business of our health care with less information than we have about caring for our pets and our house plants? The parent/child act between doctors and patients has got to come to its conclusion. It's not healthy for us!

In my earlier book, *150 Most-Asked Questions About Menopause,* I reported having been asked about my sex life by a physician for the first time when I was in my fifties. He was my new internist, not my obstetrician or gynecologist. They have never asked. Nor did my previous internist. While traveling in Sweden, I questioned a friend, a gynecologist from Hamburg, Germany, on this lack of patient/doctor communication about sex. I have asked this question often, but his answer was perhaps the most revealing of all I have received. He explained with no embarrassment that when he was a younger physician, he knew little about the subject himself and was uncomfortable discussing it with his patients, almost all of whom were older than he. Now that he is approaching his mid-sixties and most of his patients are younger than he, he is more comfortable personally with the subject. Still, he waits for them to bring it up so that he does not seem intrusive.

To some extent, he may be operating on the same premise as the doctor who didn't tell me all the side effects of medication or treatment. If we don't ask, perhaps we don't want to know. If this is the prevailing situation, then it is up to us to raise the subject, ask the questions, and get the information we need. Otherwise, the subject of sexuality carries its conversational taboo right into the doctor's office. We've got to start talking.

I was fascinated by the openness of the women in the discussion groups at my home, at the spas, and during the interviews. Most of the women did not know each other, although a few were friends or acquaintances. Yet there was almost instantaneous trust. When I questioned some of them about the level of conversational comfort that we had arrived at so quickly, they commented that trust was the keystone of intimacy. I also learned that most of us are willing to share because we are so keen to know more about ourselves through learning about other women.

136. *Why does my physician seem embarrassed when I try to discuss my sexual needs with him?*

That's an interesting and common reaction. I believe doctors are not schooled to handle or disseminate information of a sexual nature. Oh, yes, a simple yes or no answer might be forthcoming, but the insight necessary for a discussion is lacking. Some doctors tell me that it just takes too much time; others admit their own discomfort with the subject; still others are quick to state that it is not their area of expertise. With problems of a sexual nature, I think you have to seek out a physician, therapist, or counselor who specializes in sexual matters in order to get help. A list of organizations that can help you find a qualified professional in your area can be found in Appendix D.

137. Should I expect that my physician will lead me into a discussion about my lack of libido or talk about testosterone with me?

Probably not. As reported earlier in the book, the survey done by the North American Menopause Society in 1993 reported than only 16 percent of physicians had ever mentioned testosterone to their patients. The survey did not indicate whether these were female or male physicians, but only that so few were dealing with this latest information regarding libido and the ways it can be enhanced. Dr. Sandra Leiblum, professor of clinical psychiatry and codirector of the Center for Sexual and Marital Health at the Robert Woods Johnson School of Medicine, writes in *Menopause Management,* "There are two questions that your doctor should ask. 'Are you sexually active?' and 'Are you having any sexual difficulties or problems at this time?' "

138. Do you think a female physician would be better at handling a discussion of my sexual needs?

She might be, but just being female is no guarantee. When I was still vice-president of Mt. Sinai, a large teaching hospital in Cleveland, I watched with interest and hope as more and more women entered medicine. I believed for a long time that having more women physicians would solve many of the women's health problems. Now I'm not so sure that the question of disinterested medical care is gender specific. I have lectured with some marvelous, knowledgeable, compassionate female gynecologists—Doctors Sarah Berga, Mary Beard, Gloria Halverson, Deborah Nemiro, Elizabeth McClure, Wendy Buchi, and Maureen Dudgeon come to mind. I have consulted with many other professional females in the writing of my books—Doctors Estelle Ramey, Susan Lark, Jean Fourcroy, June Reinisch, Ellen Rosenblatt, and Elizabeth Stern, as well as with Candace Risen, L.I.S.W., and Deborah Grossman, R.N., to name just a few. But I have also worked with a great number of male reproductive endocrinologists, gynecologists, bone specialists, geriatric specialists, internists, and psychiatrists and psychologists who have demonstrated an equal amount of care and compassion to their patients and to our audiences. Doctors M. E. Ted Quigley, Robert Lindsay, Howard Judd, Charles Chesnut, Peter Hickox, Roger Matthews, Jon Nielson, Robert Bury, William Schlaff, Sheldon Weinstein, Steven Levine, Zachariah Newton, Stanley Althof, Chad

Deal, and Robert Butler demonstrate deep concern about all aspects of their patients' lives. So this is not a male or female physician issue, but rather a humanitarian one. Make sure that your doctor cares all about *all* of you. Discuss with your doctor his or her approach to or comfort level with sexuality counseling and help, and if you are not in the best of all patient/physician partnerships, consider looking for a new partner.

139. *Where are the doctors in all of this sex stuff? They parrot "use it or lose it": Why don't they freely discuss it?*

This demonstrates another shortfall of the health care delivery system, particularly as it affects women's issues. Yesterday's and today's doctors were not trained to care for the whole woman—with some rare exceptions noted in the training of family practice physicians. There has been intermittent discussion about the development of a medical discipline devoted to women's health. Perhaps that could be the answer to the fragmented care that we receive from adolescence onward. Perhaps not. Ask your doctor exactly what is meant by the expression "use it or lose it." Discuss any problems you have with sexual expression, from lack of desire to painful intercourse to lack of a partner. If you bring up the questions and the problems, your doctor may be willing to help you find solutions either within her or his practice or through referral to an appropriate resource. Remember that your sex drive is a component of your overall health.

140. Ever since I began hormone therapy, I am having a problem wanting sex, sex, sex. My gynecologist acknowledges the problem, but doesn't help me. What kind of a doctor should I see?

If you are on testosterone replacement therapy, then it sounds to me as if you need to have your dosage adjusted if this sexual craving is a problem for you. Your complaint is one that many midlife women would love to have, although excessive desire can be a real problem, too. One physician called testosterone replacement the "adolescence solution," indicating that for some of us, until our hormone is adjusted to just the right amount and until it levels off somewhat (which can take several months), we can become throwbacks to puberty. Excessive desire can be brought about by too much testosterone stimulation. Dr. Ramey notes that too much testosterone can engorge the clitoris.

141. Why don't doctors suggest ways for us to fulfill our sexual needs?

As written earlier in this chapter, unless they have special training in the field of human sexuality, doctors don't know a whole lot more about the subject than we do. There are a number of books listed in the Appendix as additional resources that may help you, and I suggest you begin with *The Kinsey Institute New Report on Sex,* which is a first-rate resource with a no-holds-barred style.

142. If aging and sex can go hand-in-hand, why is it that our doctors don't ask about our sex lives and our degree of sexual satisfaction?

There are a number of things that I believe your doctor should ask about every single time you have a complete physical. The first area of inquiry should be your diet—how you eat, what you eat, what you drink, and how much you drink of water, alcohol, and so on. A discussion of good nutrition should then ensue. The second is about exercise—do you do it, what kind, and how frequently. And whatever your habits, sedentary to overactive, there should be a reminder of the three kinds of exercise that are vital to good health—stretching, aerobic, and weight-bearing. The third is about sex. Are you satisfied with your sex life, what do you think is precluding a good sexual response from you, and are you having sex as frequently as you desire? It wouldn't hurt, at this point, for your doctor to offer information, assistance, and referral, if necessary.

Dr. Leiblum writes, "Although most patients believe that it is appropriate for physicians to inquire about sexual functioning, clinicians often neglect to take a sexual history."

143. *Who is the best specialist to help us with our sex problems?*

This probably depends on the nature of your problem. If lack of libido and fatigue are putting a damper on your sexual activity, the place to start would be with a gynecologist or a reproductive endocrinologist who is well versed in testosterone replacement therapy. If your problem is painful intercourse or other symptoms of menopause, she or he may be the right person to consult with as well. If your problems are with gender identity, sexual orientation, anxiety, or aversion, consider seeking the help of a psychiatrist, psychologist, therapist, or counselor who is qualified to work with mental and sexual health. If you follow the route of homeopathy or herbal medicine, see a qualified practitioner who can prescribe a remedy for you. Above all, if you have sexual problems, see someone. The prospect of achieving good sex is too good to waste.

144. *Is there any hope that in the future our doctors will begin to take a more active role in helping us with our sexual problems?*

During my interview with Dr. Robert Butler, chairman of the Department of Geriatric Medicine at the Mount Sinai School of Medicine, New York, he explained that doctors don't ask us about our sex lives because, "in the first place, they are themselves often embarrassed— strangely. Secondly, if they went to medical school before 1961, they almost certainly had no training in human sexuality. That was the first time a medical school, namely the University of Minnesota, gave a comprehensive course on human sexuality, and even today it is not clear that all 126 of our medical schools give truly comprehensive courses about the middle and later years. So a lot of the doctors are just not that well informed and not that comfortable. I think that that's not acceptable that we do not take a careful history and physical and do the appropriate tests that might be needed that bear upon sexuality. I think it's a responsibility of medicine and I hope it changes."

So what do we do in the meantime? We have to take control. We have to raise this issue with our physicians ourselves. How do we do this? Dr. Butler says, "Be straightforward and say, 'Among the various things that are important to me is the desire to preserve my sexual activity. . . . If, Doctor, you don't feel that this is within your capability, then I would appreciate your suggesting someone else.' If your doctor can't suggest someone, . . . then I'd find someone else. I suppose the most obvious choice for men is the urologist, so long as they [the doctors] aren't just thinking surgically . . . and, of course, for a woman the most obvious place to go is a gynecologist if their own primary caregiver says she or he doesn't feel capable or fails them in some way."

"The nearer we approach to the middle of life, and the better we have succeeded in entrenching ourselves in our personal standpoints and social positions, the more it appears we have discovered the right course and the right ideals and principles of behavior. For this reason we suppose them to be eternally valid, and make a virtue of unchangeably clinging to them."

—C. G. Jung
Modern Man in Search of a Soul
Harcourt Brace Jovanovich, 1933

Questions for You

1. Has your doctor ever questioned you about whether you have a satisfactory sex life?

2. Do you find yourself too embarrassed to ask your doctor to help you achieve greater sexual satisfaction?

3. If you have sexual problems, what kind of a doctor would you be most comfortable discussing them with?

4. Do you have a preference for a female or male physician?

5. Have you ever tried to discuss with your doctor changes that have occurred in your sex life?

CHAPTER 16

What Is the Real Meaning of Intimacy?

THERE IS A HUNGER in most of us for real intimacy. We reach out to others in an attempt to reach their tap-roots. We need to connect with another person in a profound way. Trust is the foundation of intimacy, and with that trust comes the responsibility for another person's vulnerable self. An intimate relationship must permit us to be candid, open, and frank. It must enable us to cast away our defenses and to relax, comfortable that we are on safe and solid ground and that we offer the same security to our partner. It is then that we can throw away our cloaks and veils, our pretenses, our airs, and be ourselves, knowing that our partner knows that this is who we are. This is the ultimate truth, the deep-seated trust, the true intimacy.

In *Sex Is Not Simple,* psychiatrist Stephen Levine tells us, "Intimacy begins with ourselves. It is a freedom to accept the entire range of our feelings and to fully experience our conflicts, paradoxes, and dilemmas. At its most basic level, intimacy is the capacity to know what exists in the privacy of our own minds."

We must love and accept ourselves before we can give love and accept the love of others fully and freely. We need to accept all facets of ourselves, including our sexual selves, if we are to realize full intimacy with our partners. If we have been capable of true intimacy in our younger years, then midlife intimacy should come more easily to us and the retirement years can bring a period of renewed intimacy, because we have more time to devote to it.

It is never too early or too late to begin the dance of intimacy, to pay attention to your partner in a deeper way, to communicate honestly and openly and to work to maintain quality in your relationships. Too often, frightened by an intimate relationship, we ward it off with ever-present work and social activities, television, and anything else that can fill the time and dull the senses with its noise to prevent us from knowing our feelings and sharing them.

Good sex requires good communication and the trust of being able to let go. The French refer to

orgasm as *le petit mort,* the little death. Allowing yourself to be brought to that small death with its attendant
release requires a letting go that is born of trust.

Now, in the AIDS-fearing 1990s, sex is being considered by some to be a religious experience, and a new
kind of therapy has evolved, a therapy that takes place
in New Age workshops. The thrust of this movement
is the sexual context as well as the sexual contact. It's
called tantric sex and is derived from the East—from
China and India—to help couples make or enrich
their emotional connections with each other. It empha-
sizes pleasing your longtime mate. Like all kinds of
marital and sexual therapy, it is about sex, love, and
intimacy.

145. *Should I expect the titillation of my youth in my forty-five-year-old marriage?*

Only if you and your mate have been particularly creative throughout the years. The loss of that kind of
electric current is sometimes the price we pay for an
exclusive long-term relationship. Yet it's not too late to
light your fires. You need to bring back variety, mystery, and spontaneity. Be adventuresome. Say "I love
you" unexpectedly. Change unlimited sexual access to
each other to more restricted access and let the antici-

pation build. Once in a while, save sex for a special occasion. Learning to arouse each other slowly, learning to break predictable sexual patterns and provide the unexpected, trying a variety of positions in a variety of places all can make sex exiting again. Many women tell me that sensuous touching is often the best part of sex. Many men report heightened enjoyment from their partners' gentle touching and massage. Experiment with each other, nurture each other, and perhaps learn erotic Eastern massage from the *Kama Sutra*. Age is the single most important predictor of how often couples make love. A key finding of a study conducted by the Society for the Scientific Study of Sex involving 6,785 married people and 678 couples who were living together was that the average frequency of sex plunges from about twelve times a month in our mid-twenties to six times a month in our mid-forties. The 1994 University of Chicago study of 3,432 Americans shows that the average American has sex once a week. It's a pity that the study only sampled persons from ages eighteen to fifty-nine, leaving out at least two decades of midlife sex. But no matter what our age, with a new marriage partner, there is definitely a "honeymoon effect" during the first year of the relationship. We may be able to re-create that effect with a long-term partner by extending our creativity into our sex lives.

146. Is it normal to feel jealous when my partner is having what appears to me to be an exciting conversation with another woman at a party?

Of course it's normal, and it demonstrates that you are not blasé about your partner. It also shows that your mate can be interesting and exciting to other women, which raises his value to you. Who would want a guy no one else was interested it? Only the most insecure among us. So let him enjoy his conversation, get turned on by your jealousy, and make sure you go home and get into bed together. That's what's important.

147. Would it be too chancy to discuss my fantasies with my partner and to ask him to join me in them?

A rich fantasy life is healthy and meaningful. If you enjoy an intimate relationship with your partner, then you yourself should know how he will react to your fantasy life. There is a risk in this kind of sharing if your fantasy involves another person or some other kind of activity that you believe will repel or revolt your partner. Try sharing bits of your fantasies at first and determine by his acceptance or rejection of them how far you can go. When I interviewed Daphne, as you may recall from Chapter 2, she told me of the wild fantasy life that came with her testosterone shots. Because of the incredible intimacy that they shared, she was able to let her husband in on what was going on in her mind, and his participation became a welcome addition to her fantasy life. It was another facet of life that they shared.

148. Sometimes I envision other partners during sexual intercourse, even though I am in love with my husband. Is that normal?

Having sex with other partners—opposite sex or same sex—is not an uncommon fantasy and in no way alters your sexual fidelity. Fantasy is just your creative mind at work, helping you to enjoy sex and to achieve orgasm.

149. Certain fears about my body continue to bother me whenever sexual activity begins. Should I try to share those fears with my partner or should I seek outside help?

The answer to this question depends largely on the nature of your relationship with your partner and the kinds of fears you are experiencing. For example, if your fears are cosmetic, having to do with your outward appearance—a bulging belly, droopy breasts, or a sagging bottom—and you and your partner are truly intimate, consider verbalizing these concerns. You may be happily surprised to learn that your partner is not as hung up on the wrappings as you seem to be, but is much more interested in the contents. Reassurance in this regard can work wonders in helping you to reappraise your body image and reduce your fears. If, however, your concerns are medical in nature, having to do with a past or present illness or abuse, it is important to get help so that you can deal with these fears effectively.

150. Now that scientific research has shown that a woman who is healthy at fifty may live well into her mid-eighties or beyond, how should she integrate the idea of other partners into her longer life?

I grew up in the fifties. Then we thought you waited until marriage to have sexual intercourse and that your mate was your sex partner for life. Some women and men had no other sexual experience prior to their marriage and certainly none other during their long lives together. Then, suddenly, through divorce or widowhood, some find themselves alone. Other women have had premarital and extramarital experiences, but then may have settled into an exclusive long-term relationship as well. They, too, may find themselves alone. Now, with a long stretch of healthy years that we may be fortunate enough to have ahead of us, we have to decide how we will spend the bonus years. Some women choose celibacy; others want temporary partners; still others want a chance at another exclusive relationship. The tendency seems to be that we choose to repeat a good experience. And if we choose other partners as we age, we must come to terms with the fact that we are not being unfaithful to other people or to their memories. We are, quite simply, getting on with and enjoying our lives.

At midlife, we are not concerned about the death of our youth, but rather we stand on the brink of an enjoyable second adulthood, buoyed by our newfound maturity.

I find that my own midlife transition has brought a remarkable closeness and caring into my long-term marriage. It is as if we are now each clearly defined and thus able to understand and appreciate each other in a new way. Irrevocably linked, we have become individually sound.

A Final Note:
Write to Me,
Talk to Me

WHEN I FINISHED writing *150 Most-Asked Questions About Menopause,* the batch of questions for which there hadn't been sufficient space bothered me greatly. So I began opening lines of communication with my readers via the "Write to Me, Talk to Me" section of the book. Thousands of women responded. They wrote, they called, questions poured in, and I tried to answer those that were appropriate in *150 Most-Asked Questions About Osteoporosis,* which was published in the fall of 1993.

With 300 pressing questions already answered in the two books, I continued my open lines and you continued to write. This book, the third in the 150 Most-Asked Questions series, brings that number to 450 most-asked questions and answers. I am delighted to hear from my readers and to help them if I am able, and many of us have stayed in touch. That's good, because you let me know what women's health issue you want me to tackle next. You also added immeasurably to the bank of information from women that I have been building.

Happily, many of you have attended my seminars and lectures and have come to meet me in person. What a thrill it is when pen and ink turn into flesh and blood. I hope you will continue to write, share your comments and suggestions, and ask your questions.

We all know that no one can answer specific medical questions by mail or phone and that taking care of a medical need requires a personal visit to your own health-care provider, be she or he an allopathic or alternative medicine specialist. If you are searching for your own "Doctor Right," please look in the Appendix for the organization that can assist you in finding a practitioner in your area.

If you want to stay in touch and share your thoughts and ideas with me in the hope of helping other women maximize the second half of adult life, you can reach me at the following address:

Ruth S. Jacobowitz
5 Longmeadow Lane
Cleveland, Ohio 44122

Also, if you wish to help me by providing information for my next book, please contact me and I will send you a short questionnaire that you can fill out and return. Thank you for joining my consumer research project that is designed to continue to learn and to share "what women really want to know."

—*Ruth S. Jacobowitz*

Appendix A

Recommended Reading and References

Atkins, Robert C., M.D. *Dr. Atkins' Health Revolution*. Boston: Houghton Mifflin, 1988.

Barbach, Lonnie, Ph.D., and David Geisinger, Ph.D. *Going the Distance*. New York: Doubleday, 1991.

Benson, Herbert, M.D. *The Mind/Body Effect*. New York: Berkley Books, 1979.

Berg, Goran M.D., Ph.D. and Mats Hammar, M.D., Ph.D., eds. *The Modern Management of The Menopause:* The Proceedings of the VII International Congress on The Menopause, Stockholm, Sweden 1993. Pearl River, New York: Parthenon, 1994.

Boston Women's Health Book Collective, The. *The New Our Bodies, Ourselves.* New York: Simon & Schuster, 1984.

Brecher, Edward M., and the Editors of Consumer Reports Books. *Love, Sex & Aging.* Mt. Vernon, New York: Consumers Union of United States, 1984.

Bricklin, Mark. *The Practical Encyclopedia of Natural Healing.* New York: Penguin Books, 1990.

Burger, H. and M. Boulet, eds. *A Portrait of the Menopause.* Park Ridge, New Jersey: Parthenon, 1991.

Burton Goldberg Group. *Alternative Medicine: The Definitive Guide.* Puyallup, Washington: Future Medicine Publishing, 1993.

Butler, Robert N., M.D. and Myrna I. Lewis, M.S.W. *Love and Sex After 60.* New York: Ballantine Books/Random House, 1993.

Cole, Ellen, Ph.D. "Lesbians at Menopause." *A Friend Indeed Newsletter* 9, no. 9 (February 1993).

Comfort, Alex, M.D., D.Sc. *The New Joy of Sex.* New York: Crown, 1991.

Chopra, Deepak, M.D. *Ageless Body, Timeless Mind.* New York: Harmony Books/Crown, 1993.

Cutler, Winnifred B., Ph.D. *Hysterectomy: Before & After.* New York: Harper & Row, 1988.

Doress, Paula Brown, and Diana Laskin Siegal. *Ourselves, Growing Older.* New York: Simon & Schuster, 1987.

Eid, J. Francois, M.D., and Carol A. Pearce. *Making Love Again.* New York: Brunner/Mazel, 1993.

Fast, Julian, *Body Language.* New York: Pocket Books, 1971.

Freedman, Rita, Ph.D. *Bodylove.* New York: Harper & Row, 1988.

Friday, Nancy. *Women on Top.* New York: Simon & Schuster, 1991.

Friedan, Betty. *The Feminine Mystique.* New York: W.W. Norton, 1983.

Gannon, Linda, Ph.D. "Sexual Activity as a Choice." *A Friend Indeed Newsletter* 9, no. 8 (January, 1994).

Greer, Germaine. *The Change.* New York: Alfred A. Knopf, 1992.

Hausman, Patricia, and Judith Benn Hurley. *The Healing Foods.* Emmaus, Pennsylvania: Rodale Press, 1989.

Hayes, Christopher L., Ph.D., Deborah Anderson, and Melinda Blau. *Our Turn: The Good News About Women and Divorce.* New York: Pocket Books, 1993.

Heyn, Dalma. *The Erotic Silence of the American Wife.* New York: Turtle Bay Books/Random House, 1992.

Hite, Shere. *The Hite Report.* New York: Macmillan, 1976.

In Health "The No-Gimmick Weight-Loss Plan." (December/January 1992): 82–83.

Jacobowitz, Ruth S. *150 Most-Asked Questions About Menopause.* New York: Hearst Books, 1993.

Jacobowitz, Ruth S. *150 Most-Asked Questions About Osteoporosis.* New York: Hearst Books, 1993.

Janus, Samuel S., Ph.D., and Cynthia L. Janus, M.D. *The Janus Report on Sexual Behavior.* New York: John Wiley, 1993.

Kinsey, Alfred C., Wardell Pomeroy, and Clyde E. Martin. *Sexual Behavior in the Human Male.* Philadelphia: W. B. Saunders, 1948.

Kinsey, Alfred C., Wardell Pomeroy, Clyde E. Martin, and Paul M. Gebhard. *Sexual Behavior in the Human Female.* Philadelphia: W. B. Saunders, 1955.

Laumann, Edward, Robert Michael, Stuart Michaels, et al. *The Social Organization of Sexuality.* Chicago: University of Chicago Press, 1994.

Leiblum, Sandra, and Raymond Rosen, eds. *Principles and Practice of Sex Therapy: Update for the 1990s.* New York: Guilford Press, 1989.

Levine, Stephen B., M.D. *Sex Is Not Simple.* Columbus, Ohio: Ohio Psychology Publishing, 1988.

Levinson, Daniel J., et al. *The Seasons of a Man's Life.* New York: Alfred A. Knopf, 1978.

Lobo, Rogerio A., M.D., ed. *Treatment of the Postmenopausal Woman: Basic and Clinical Aspects.* New York: Raven Press, 1994.

Lockie, Dr. Andrew. *The Family Guide to Homeopathy.* New York. Fireside/Simon & Schuster, 1994.

MacLean Helene, ed., with D. S. Thompson, *EveryWoman's Health,* 4th ed., New York: Doubleday Book and Music Clubs, GuildAmerica Books, 1990.

Masters, William H., M.D., and Virginia E. Johnson. *Human Sexual Response.* Boston: Little Brown, 1966.

Masters, William H., M.D., Virginia E. Johnson, and Robert C. Kolodny, M.D. *Heterosexuality.* HarperCollins: New York, 1994.

Mindell, Earl, R.Ph., Ph.D., and Carol Colman. *Earl Mindell's Herb Bible.* New York: Fireside/Simon & Schuster, 1992.

Morgan, Dr. Brian L.G., and Roberta Morgan. *Hormones: How They Affect Behavior, Metabolism, Growth, Development and Relationships.* Los Angeles: The Body Press, 1989.

Morris, Desmond. *Intimate Behaviour.* New York: Random House, 1971.

Rodale Health Staff, eds. "Sex: What's in the Future," in *Future Youth.* Emmaus, Pennsylvania: Rodale Press, 1987.

Reinisch, June M., Ph.D., with Ruth Beasley, M.L.S. *The Kinsey Institute New Report on Sex.* New York: St. Martin's Press, 1990.

Rosenthal, Saul H., M.D. *Sex Over Forty.* New York: Putnam, 1987.

Rubenstein, Carin, Ph.D. "The American Health Sex Survey." *American Health* (December 1991): 56–57.

Sheehy, Gail. *Passages.* New York: Bantam Books, 1974.

Shephard, Bruce D., M.D., and Carroll A. Shephard, R.N., Ph.D. *The Complete Guide to Women's Health,* 2nd ed. New York: Plume/Penguin Books USA, 1990.

Shock, Nathan W.; Richard C. Greulich; Reubin Andres; David Arenberg; Paul T. Costa, Jr.; Edward G. Lakatta and Jordan D. Tobin. *Normal Human Aging: The Baltimore Longitudinal Study of Aging.* U.S. Department of Health and Human Services, 1984.

Sinclair, Brett Jason. *Alternative Health Care Resources.* New York: Parker Publishing, Prentice-Hall, 1992.

Steinem, Gloria. "Erotica vs. Pornography: A Clear and Present Difference." In Laura Lederer, ed. *Take Back the Night: Women on Pornography.* New York: William Morrow, 1980.

Steinem, Gloria. *Outrageous Acts and Everyday Rebellions.* New York: Holt Rinehart and Winston, 1983.

Tapley, Donald F., M.D.; Thomas Q. Morris, M.D.; Lewis P. Rowland, M.D.; and Robert J. Weiss, M.D. *The Columbia University College of Physicians and Surgeons Complete Home Medical Guide.* New York: Crown, 1989.

U.S. Department of Health and Human Services, Public Health Service, and National Institutes of Health. *The Menopause Time of Life.* NIH Publication No. 86-2461. (For copies of this publication, write to: NIH Information Center, 2209 Distribution Circle, Silver Spring, MD, 20910.)

U.S. Department of Health and Human Services, Public Health Service, and National Institutes of Health. *Older & Wiser—The Baltimore Longitudinal Study of Aging.* September 1989. NIH Publication No. 89-2797.

University of California, Berkeley. *The Wellness Encyclopedia.* Boston: Houghton Mifflin, 1991.

Utian, Wulf H., M.D., Ph.D., and Ruth S. Jacobowitz. *Managing Your Menopause.* New York: Prentice-Hall, 1990.

Westheimer, Ruth. *Dr. Ruth's Guide to Good Sex.* New York: Warner Books, 1983.

Whipple, Beverly, Ph.D., R.N., and Gina Ogden, Ph.D. *Safe Encounters.* New York: McGraw-Hill, 1989.

Wolf, Naomi. *The Beauty Myth.* New York: William Morrow, 1991.

$Appendix\ B$

$Other\ Professional\ Sources$

"Alcoholism as a Public Health Problem." *NIH News and Features* (Summer 1993), pp. 22–23.

Attitudes of Gender Differences Survey Conducted by CNN, *USA Today,* and the Gallup Organization, 1993.

Based on a survey by Louis Harris and Associates. "Commonwealth Fund Survey of Women's Health, The." February and March 1993. July 14, 1993.

"Condom for Women, A." *Berkeley Wellness Letter* 8, no. 11 (August 1992), pp. 6–7.

"Desire in the Sexual Crucible." *Contemporary Sexuality: Newsletter of the American Association of Sex Educators, Counselors and Therapists* 27, no. 4 (April 1993), pp. 1–4.

Donovan, Patricia. *Testing Positive: Sexually Transmitted Diseases and the Public Health Response.* New York: The Alan Guttmacher Institute, 1993.

Elias, Marilyn. "Late-Life Love." *Harvard Health Letter* 18, no. 1 (November 1992): pp. 1–3.

"Exercises That Cure Impotence." *Edell Health Letter* 11, no. 9 (October 1993), p. 6, from *British Journal of Urology* 7, n.a. (1993), pp. 52–57.

"How Effective Are Condoms?" *Berkeley Wellness Letter* 9, no. 4 (December 1992), p. 6.

"Impotence." *NIH Consensus Statement* 10, no. 4 (December 7–9, 1992), pp. 1–29.

"Impotence Treatments Jazz Up Marriage." *Edell Health Letter* 11, no. 9 (October 1992), p. 6.

Leiblum, Sandra Risa, Ph.D. "Libido and Lubrication: Tips for Sexuality Counseling." *Menopause Management* 2, no. 3 (March 1993), pp. 16–18.

MacBride, Gail. "Postmenopausal Hormone-Replacement Therapy: A Special Report." *Harvard Health Letter* (October 1993).

Matthews, Karen A., et al. "Influences of Natural Menopause on Psychological Characteristics and Symptoms of Middle-Aged Healthy Women." *Journal of Consulting and Clinical Psychology* 58, no. 3 (1990), pp. 345–351.

National Institute on Aging. "Controlling Urinary Incontinence." *Clinical Bulletin* (1993), pp. 1–2.

————. "Sexuality in Later Life." *Age Page,* pp. 1–2. Department of Health and Human Services, 1992.

————. "Special Report on Aging, 1993: Older Americans Can Expect to Live Longer and Healthier Lives," pp. 1–28. (NIH 93-3409).

————. "Urinary Incontinence." *Age Page* (1992), pp. 1–2.

National Women's Health Network Staff, eds. *Taking Hormones and Women's Health: Choices, Risks and Benefits,* 3rd ed. Washington, D.C.: National Women's Health Network, 1993.

Rudy, David R., M.D. "Postgraduate Medicine: A Special Report." *Hormone Replacement Therapy* 88, no. 8 (December 1990), pp. 157–164.

Sarrel, Philip M., M.D. "Sexuality and Menopause." *Obstetrics & Gynecology* 75, no. 4 (April 1990 Supplement), pp. 26s–35s.

————. and M. I. Whitehead, M.D. "Sex and Menopause: Defining the Issues." *Maturitas* 7, no. 3 (September 1985), pp. 217–224.

Shanoff, Carolyn S. "Bladder Training Reduces Incontinence in Older Women." *Healthline,* National Institutes of Health (1991), pp. 1–3.

Simons, Wallace R., Ph.D. "Male Menopause: Fact or Myth?" *Women's Health Connections* 1, no. 2 (June/July 1993).

"Special Issue: 25 Years of Hormone Replacement Therapy." *Maturitas* 12, no. 3 (September 1990), pp. 159–319.

Speroff, Leon, M.D., et al. *Androgens in the Menopause: Symposium Proceedings.* New York: BMI/McGraw-Hill, 1988.

"Taking a Woman's Sex Life Seriously." *Edell Health Letter* (December 1993/January 1994): p. 5, from *The Female Patient* 18, n.a. (July 1993), p. 35.

"Treating Affairs in the Sexual Crucible." *Contemporary Sexuality: Newsletter of the American Association of Sex Educators, Counselors and Therapists* 27, no. 9 (September 1993): pp. 1–4.

"Truth About Latex Condoms: A SEICUS Fact Sheet, The." *SEICUS Report* 22, no. 1 (October/November 1993), pp. 17–19.

Appendix C

Other Sources

Althof, Dr. Stanley. "Sexual Fantasies Usually Harmless." *Cleveland Plain Dealer,* July 6, 1993.

Altman, Lawrence K. "A Study on Impotence Suggests Half of Men over 40 May Have Problem." *The New York Times,* December 22, 1993.

———. "U.S. Finds 550,000 Are Infected with H.I.V. Outside Risk Groups." *The New York Times,* December 14, 1993.

Angier, Natalie. "Marriage Is a Lifesaver for Men After 45." *The New York Times,* October 16, 1990.

Bakos, Susan Crain. "Plague of Routine Sex." *Cosmopolitan* (March 1993), pp. 151–153.

Barringer, Felicity. "Among Elderly, Men's Prospects Are the Brighter." *The New York Times,* November 1, 1992.

———. "Measuring Sexuality Through Polls Can Be Shaky." *The New York Times,* April 25, 1993.

Beck, Melinda. "The New Middle Age." *Newsweek* (December 7, 1992), pp. 50–56.

———, with Karen Springen, Donna Foote, and bureau reports. "Sex Psychotherapy Doctors Sleeping With Patients: A Growing Crisis of Ethical Abuse." *Newsweek* (April 13, 1992), pp. 53–57.

Berendt, John. "The Orgasm Reconsidered." *Esquire* (June 1993), pp. 27, 29.

Berger, Amy. "Erotic Mistakes." *Complete Woman* (February 1994), p. 10.

Chartrand, Sabra. "A Female Condom, Attached to Underwear to Prevent AIDS." "Patents" by Sabra Chartrand, *The New York Times,* January 31, 1994.

Chethik, Neil. "Living the Single Life Without Sex." *Cleveland Plain Dealer,* August 23, 1993.

Cooper, Joel R. "Vaginal Fitness, Hotter Sex, Healthier Women." *Longevity* (March 1993), p. 4.

Crichton, Sarah. "Sexual Correctness." *Newsweek* (October 25, 1993), pp. 52–58.

Darling, Lynne. "As Customers Age, Marketers Discover New Notion of Beauty." *The New York Times,* January 24, 1994.

Dithridge, Lisa, and Stephen O'Shea. "Men: Give Them a Break or the Boot." *Elle* (May 1993): p. 76.

Elias, Marilyn. "Age of Intimacy: Older Couples Slow Down a Bit." *USA Today,* November 5, 1993.

Foote, Jennifer. "Holding Disease at Bay as Lives Lengthen." *Cleveland Plain Dealer,* December 5, 1993.

Friedan, Betty. "My Quest for the Fountain of Age." *Time* (September 6, 1993), pp. 61–64.

Haddon, Genia Pauli, D.Min., Ph.D. "Sex, Self & Spirit." *Spectrum—The Whollistic News Magazine* (January/ February 1994).

Harris, Lynn. "Twenty-five Ways to Make Your Marriage Sexier." *Ladies Home Journal* (May 1993), pp. 88–89.

Janus, Samuel S., Ph.D., and Cynthia L. Janus, M.D. "The Janus Report: Other Peoples' Sex Lives" (Reprinted from *The Janus Report on Sexual Behavior*). *Redbook* (March 1993), pp. 69–71.

Kent, Debra. "Too Tired for Sex." *Cleveland Plain Dealer*, December 8, 1992.

Kirn, Walter. "Heavy Breathing." *Mirabella* (March 1993), p. 50.

Kohnhorst, Keith. "Seeking Spiritual Health." *Natural Health* (March/April 1993), pp. 86, 87, 131.

Kolata, Gina. "New Views on Life Spans Alter Forecasts on Elderly." *The New York Times,* November 16, 1992.

Kuriansky, Judy, Ph.D. "Pillow Talk." *Ladies Home Journal* (January 1994), pp. 52–59.

Landers, Ann. "Ann Gets Unexpected Response to Controversial Column." *Miami Herald,* November 28, 1993.

Maynard, Joyce. "Sex and the Single Mom." *Redbook* (March 1993), p. 34.

McCleery, Kathleen. "The No-Gimmick Weight-Loss Plan." *In Health* (December/January 1992), pp. 82–83.

Murray, Linda. "Love and Longevity." *Longevity* (September 1993), pp. 30, 69, 70.

———. "The Love Diet." *Longevity* (December 1993), p. 20.

———. "Love Hormones." *Longevity* (February 1993), p. 32.

Nadler, Holly. "My Life as a Man." *Lear's* (December 1993): p. 60.

Naughton, Ena. "Middle Age Is Growing Ever Older." *Miami Herald*, February 4, 1990.

Nemy, Enid. "Widows Are Choosing Independent New Lives Rather Than Marriages." *The New York Times,* June 18, 1992.

Noonan, Peggy. "Coming Soon: Testosterone Replacement." *Longevity* (January 1994), p. 28.

"No Place Like Home." *AARP Bulletin* 34, no. 8 (September 1993).

"Panel Says Impotency Can Be Treated." *Cleveland Plain Dealer,* December 10, 1992.

Pollan, Stephen M., and Mark Levine. "The Graying Yuppie." *New York* (March 9, 1992), pp. 28–37.

Rubinstein, Carin, Ph.D. "Sex: The Ultimate Survey." *Mademoiselle* (June 1993), pp. 130–137.

"Survey: What You Told Us, The." Co-sponsored by the Center for Women Policy Studies. *Mirabella* (June 1993), pp. 133–140.

Utian, Wulf H., M.D., and Isaac Schiff, M.D. "NAMS-Gallup Survey on Women's Knowledge, Information Sources, and Attitudes to Menopause and Hormone Replacement Therapy." *Menopause: Journal of the North American Menopause Society* 1, no. 1 (Spring 1994), pp. 39–48.

Vogt, Jenny. "Celibacy in Marriage Is Not Unusual, Authors Say." *Cleveland Plain Dealer,* August 29, 1993.

Vukovic, Laurel. "Enhancing Female Sexual Response." *Natural Health* (March/April 1993), pp. 59–61.

Wachter, Susan. "Help for Lackluster Libidos." *Longevity* (February 1994), pp. 92–93.

Wolf, Naomi. "Radical Heterosexuality." *Ms.* (July/August 1992), pp. 1–3.

"Women Downplay Risk of Sex-Related Disease, Survey Finds." *Miami Herald,* February 15, 1994.

Papers Presented

Bachmann, Gloria, M.D. "Sexuality: The Role of Declining Gonadal Hormones." The North American Menopause Society 2nd Annual Meeting, September 25–28, 1991; Montreal, Canada.

Barrett-Connor, Elizabeth, M.D. "Estrogen and Cancer." The North American Menopause Society 2nd Annual Meeting, September 25–28, 1991; Montreal, Canada.

Pike, Malcolm, M.D. "Achieving Progestin Benefits at Minimal Risks." The North American Menopause Society 2nd Annual Meeting, September 25–28, 1991; Montreal, Canada.

Sarrel, Philip, M.D. "Sex and Menopause." The North American Menopause Society 2nd Annual Meeting, September 25–28, 1991; Montreal, Canada.

Whitehead, Malcolm, M.D. "The Use and Misuse of Progestogens." The North American Menopause Society 2nd Annual Meeting, September 25–28, 1991; Montreal, Canada.

Appendix D

Self-Help Resources

Action on Smoking and Health (ASH)
2013 H Street, N.W.
Washington, D.C. 20006

American Association of Naturopathic Physicians
P.O. Box 20386
Seattle, Washington 98102

American Association of Retired Persons (AARP)
1909 K Street, N.W.
Washington, D.C. 20049

American Association of Sex Educators, Counselors and
   Therapists
11 Dupont Circle, N.W., Suite 220
Washington, DC 20036
1-202-462-1171 for help in finding a sex therapist.

American Botanical Council
P.O. Box 201660
Austin, Texas 78720

American Cancer Society
1599 Clifton Road
Atlanta, Georgia 30329

American Dental Association
Department of Public Information and Education
211 E. Chicago Avenue
Chicago, Illinois 60611

American Diabetes Association
National Service Center
1660 Duke Street
Alexandria, Virginia 22314
Call toll free: 1-800-232-3472

American Foundation for the Blind
15 West 16th Street
New York, New York 10011

American Heart Association
7320 Greenville Avenue
Dallas, Texas 75231

American Holistic Medical Association
2002 Eastlake Avenue East
Seattle, Washington 98102

American Lung Association
1740 Broadway, P.O. Box 596
New York, New York 10019-4374

American Society of Plastic & Reconstructive Surgeons
233 N. Michigan Avenue, #1900
Chicago, Illinois 60601

Bajamar Women's Healthcare
9609 Dielman Rock Island
St. Louis, Missouri 63132
1-800-255-8025

Belmar Pharmacy
12860 West Cedar Drive, Suite 210
Lakewood, Colorado 80228
1-800-525-9473

Cancer Information Service
(A program of the National Cancer Institute)
National Cancer Institute
9000 Rockville Pike
Building 31, Room 10A24
Bethesda, Maryland 20892
Call toll free: 1-800-4-CANCER

College Pharmacy
833 North Tejon Street
Colorado Springs, Colorado 80903
1-800-888-9358

Elderhostel
100 Boylston Street, Suite 200
Boston, Massachusetts 02116
(Educational experiences for older adults on campuses
throughout the country)

Female Urologists, to locate write:
Jean Fourcroy, M.D., Ph.D.
6310 Swords' Way
Bethesda, Maryland 20817

Help for Incontinent People
P.O. Box 544A
Union, South Carolina 29379

Herb Research Foundation
1007 Pearl Street, Suite 200
Boulder, Colorado 80302

Homeopathic Academy of Naturopathic Physicians
14653 Graves Road
Mulino, Oregon 97042

Homeopathic Educational Services
2124 Kittredge Street
Berkeley, California 94704

Impotence Anonymous
119 S. Ruth Street
Maryville, Tennessee 37801-5746
(Write and ask for a chapter near you. Send a self-addressed stamped envelope.)

Impotence Information Center
P.O. Box 9, Department USA
Minneapolis, Minnesota 55440
1-800-843-4315, to find a support group in your area.

International Foundation for Homepathy
2366 Eastlake Avenue East, Suite 301
Seattle, Washington 98102

National Center for Homeopathy
1500 Massachusetts Avenue, N.W., Suite 42
Washington, D.C. 20005

National Council on the Aging (NCOA)
600 Maryland Avenue, S.W. West Wing 100
Washington, D.C. 20024

National Council on Alcoholism
1151 K Street N.W., Suite 320
Washington, D.C. 20005

National Eye Care Project
American Academy of Ophthalmology
P.O. Box 6988
San Francisco, California 94120-6988
Call toll free: 1-800-222-EYES

National Institute on Aging (NIA)
Information Center
P.O. Box 8057
Gaithersburg, Maryland 20898-8057

National Institute of Arthritis and Musculoskeletal and
 Skin Diseases
NIAMS Clearinghouse
Box AMS
Bethesda, Maryland 20892

National Institutes of Health
Federal Building, Room 6C12
Bethesda, Maryland 20205

National Kidney and Urologic Diseases Information
 Clearinghouse
P.O. Box NKUDIC
Bethesda, Maryland 20892

The National Osteoporosis Foundation
2100 M Street N.W.
Suite 602, Dept. V.F.
Washington, D.C. 20037

National Society to Prevent Blindness
500 E. Remington Road
Schaumburg, Illinois 60173

North American Menopause Society
c/o University Hospital
Department of Ob/Gyn
2074 Abington Road
Cleveland, Ohio 44106

Office on Smoking and Health
5600 Fishers Lane
Park Bldg., Room 1–10
Rockville, Maryland 20857

Sex Information and Education Council of United States
80 Fifth Avenue, Suite 801
New York, New York 10011

Sexuality Library
San Francisco, California
Mail Order Catalogue: books on sexual facts, sexual politics, and erotica. Videotapes as well.
(415) 974-8990

The Skin Cancer Foundation
245 Fifth Avenue, Suite 2402
New York, New York 10016

Women's International Pharmacy
5708 Monona Drive
Madison, Wisconsin 53716-3152
1-800-279-5708

Newsletters & Magazines

A Friend Indeed
Box 515
Place du Parc Station
Montreal, Canada H2W 2P1
(514) 843-5730

Menopause News
2074 Union Street
San Francisco, California
1-800-241-MENO

Midlife Woman
5129 Logan Avenue South
Minneapolis, Minnesota 55419-1019
1-612-925-0020

Sex After Forty
P.O. Box 1600
Chapel Hill, North Carolina 27515

Éternelle (the magazine celebrating woman in midlife)
P.O. Box 1646
Los Altos, California 94023-1646

Index

acne, 68, 104
adrenal glands, testosterone
    production in, 33, 34, 64, 65,
    102–103, 179
Ageless Body, Timeless Mind
    (Chopra), 202
aggressive behavior, 68, 104, 160
AIDS, 161, 227–230, 237
    extramarital affairs and, 152,
    153
    see also HIV virus
alcohol, 48, 54, 141
    sexual inhibitions and, 208
    sleep problems and, 76
    testosterone and, 110
Allen, Woody, 83
Alman, Isadora, 177
alternative therapies, 48, 66, 69
    herbs, 76, 134, 173, 214–215
    Vitamin E and, 75–76, 134
Althof, Stanley, 47, 142–143, 244
Anderson, Deborah, 157
androgens, 32, 34
    see also testosterone

andropause (male menopause;
    viropause), 97–98, 110, 111
androstenedione, 102
anger, 91, 133
anxiety, 80, 91, 110, 141
    drugs and, 50–51, 119
    male performance, 97, 142, 178
    menopause and, 8
Any Woman's Blues (Jong), 225
aphrodisiacs, 106, 206–207,
    214–215
arteries, hardening of, 119
Arteriosclerosis and Thrombosis,
    103
artichoke hearts, 215
asparagus, 212, 215
Astroglide, 64, 96, 122
Australia, testosterone therapy in,
    107
awakenings, 78, 82–83

Bachman, Gloria, 172
Bajamar Women's Health Care,
    67, 172, 180

baldness, male-pattern, 104
Baltimore Longitudinal Study on
    Aging, 98
Basic Instinct (movie), 183
baths, bathing, 83, 125, 186–187
Beard, Mary, 244
Beasley, Ruth, 220
Beatty, Warren, xxiv
Becoming Orgasmic (video),
    175–176
bee pollen, 76
Belmar Pharmacy, 67, 171–172,
    180
Berga, Sarah, 244
Better Sex Video Series, 175
bilateral oopherectomy, 34, 66–67,
    72–73
biofeedback computers, 199
birth control pill, 79
bladder control problems, 5
Blau, Melinda, 157
bloating, progestin and, 66
blood pressure, high
    (hypertension), 50, 119,
    140–141, 142
blood tests, 60, 90, 95–96
body image, 48, 82, 85–87,
    125–126
    diet and, 204–206, 208–209
    exercise and, 82, 87, 125, 200
    intimacy and, 257–258
body language, 182–183
Body Language (Fast), 183
Bodylove (Freedman), 86
Bombeck, Erma, 190
boredom, sexual, *see* sexual
    boredom, avoiding
brain:
    erections and, 140
    hypothalamus of, 32, 134
    night sweats and, 134
    ovaries and, 32–33, 64
    pituitary gland and, 33, 64, 102

sex and, 62–63, 80, 86, 125
breasts:
    cancer of, 105, 172
    sensitivity of, 69
Bridges of Madison County, The
    (Waller), 79
Brown, Helen Gurley, 113–114
bubble baths, 83, 125, 186–187
Buchi, Wendy, 244
Buck, Pearl S., 148
Bury, Robert, 244
Butler, Robert, 98, 110, 141, 219,
    245, 249–250

Cabin Fever (video), 202
calcium, 68, 174, 206
Campion, Jane, 159
cancer:
    breast, 105, 172
    endometrial, 66, 171, 174
    prostate, 103, 111
cardiovascular disease (heart
    disease), 67, 104, 172
    testosterone therapy and,
        103–104, 120–122, 172
caressing, 135, 159–160
Carruthers, Malcolm, 110–111
celibacy, 88–89, 100
Change, The (Greer), xxi–xxii
chasteberry (*Vitex*), 207, 214
Chesnut, Charles, 244
Chetnik, Neil, 89
Chicago University of, 88, 105,
    255
child abuse, 25–26, 63
Chinese herbs, 76, 214–215
cholesterol, 103, 214
Chopra, Deepak, 202
Cleveland *Plain Dealer*, 89
clitoris, xi, xxiv, 223, 246
clothes, sexy, 60–61, 125, 126, 183,
    188–189
clover, red or purple, 173

collagen injections, 139
College Pharmacy, 67, 172, 180
Comfort, Alex, 46, 201
"Commentary on Current
    Trends in Sex Therapy"
    (Yaffe), 123
communication, 129–149
  as alternative to affairs,
    154–155
  in cars, 178
  about different goals, 135
  doctor-patient, 73, 116, 118,
    119–120, 241–250
  importance of, xi, 12, 41,
    129–133
  intimacy and, 253
  in lesbian relationships, 29–30,
    130
  about male sexual dysfunction,
    139–148
  about night sweats, 133–135
  nonverbal, *see* body language
  problems in, 9–10, 99–100, 116,
    118, 119–120
  of sexual needs, 136–137, 155,
    178, 230
  about stress incontinence,
    137–139
  therapy and, 146–147
  video guidelines and, 176
companionship, 94, 132
Company (TV show), 113–114
condoms, 162, 163, 225, 228
  fellatio and, 50
  female, 163–164
  putting on, 235–236
Constructing the Sexual Crucible
    (Schnarch), 84
cosmetic surgery, 86
counseling, 41–42, 147, 154, 248
Crichton, Michael, 232
cuddling, 135
cunnilingus, 49

*Current Trends in Treatment in
    Psychiatry*, 123
Cutler, Winnifred, 72–73

Damiana, 173, 215
dating, 161–162
  adult children and, 234–235
Deal, Chad, 244–245
depression, 23, 24, 91
  drugs and, 50–51, 119
  estrogen and, 171
  overweight and, 210
  progestin and, 66, 171, 173–174
desire, *see* sexual desire
diabetes, 50, 119, 140, 142
diaphragms, 225
diet, 48, 82, 204–216
  body image and, 204–206,
    208–209
  calcium in, 174, 206
  carbohydrates in, 207
  diuretics and, 212
  fat in, 86, 126, 174
  herbs and, 214–215
  nutritional deficiencies and,
    141
  overweight and, 210, 211–212
  raw oysters and, 207
  sexual desire and, 213–214
  water retention and, 210–213
Disclosure (Crichton), 232
diuretics, 212
doctors, *see* physicians; *specific
    specialists*
Dudgeon, Maureen, 244
Donahue (TV show), 10
Donovan, Patricia, 229
drugs, 48
  depression and, 50–51, 119
  impotence and, 50, 141, 142,
    147
  sexual desire and, 50–51, 119
Dychtwald, Ken, 205

Eat More, Weigh Less (Ornish), 215

eggs, 32, 33

ejaculation, xi, 91
  aging and, 71, 80, 97, 223
  fellatio and, 50
  testosterone and, 65

Ellerbee, Linda, 77

Elvira Madigan (movie), 192–193

emotion, orgasm and, 84

emotional satisfaction, 94, 132

empty nest syndrome, 97

endocrinologists, 248

endometrial cancer, 66, 171, 174

endorphins, 125, 174, 184
  exercise and, 194, 197

erection, xi, 91
  aging and, 48, 71, 80, 97, 223
  fellatio and, 49–50
  massage and, 187
  in men over fifty, 48, 71
  penile implants and, 144–145
  penile injections and, 145–146
  penile vacuums and, 143–144
  problems with, 9, 11, 48, 97, 136, 139–146
  testosterone and, 65

erotica, pornography vs., 122–124

Erotic Silence of the American Wife, The (Heyn), 93

ERT, *see* estrogen replacement therapy

Estratest, 68, 108–109, 117, 119

estrogen, 31–33, 64, 171, 179
  breast cancer and, 105, 172
  lack of, 4, 10, 53, 63–64, 69, 72
  natural, 172–173
  puberty and, 32
  sexual desire and, 65, 72, 96, 109
  skin and, 53, 69

estrogen cream, 64

estrogen replacement therapy (ERT), 11, 23, 54, 59, 60, 66, 96
  hot flashes and, 75, 134
  hysterectomy and, 66
  night sweats and, 134
  progestin and, 67
  stress incontinence and, 138
  testosterone therapy and, 117–118, 120–121, 172
  vaginal lubrication and, 122
  water retention and, 212

Éternelle, 3

ethics and politics, sexual, 227–239
  adult children and, 234–235
  AIDS and STDS and, 227–230
  communication and, 230
  condoms and, 235–236
  extramarital sex and, 237–238
  lesbian relationships and, 238
  objectification and, 234
  prostitutes and, 236–237
  retirement communities and, 236
  senior adults and, 231
  sexually explicit materials and, 231–232
  social correctness and, 232–233

evening primrose oil, 76, 214–215

exercise, 48, 192–203
  aerobic, 193–194
  body image and, 82, 87, 125, 200
  empowerment and, 194
  endorphins and, 194, 197
  Kegel, 138, 198–200
  requirements for, 193
  sexual desire and, 123, 192–202
  sleep problems and, 76
  sluggishness and, 200–201
  weight-bearing, 193, 194

extramarital affairs, 152–155, 237–238

communication and, 154–155
incidence of, 152–154
secrecy about, 162
eyes, sex signals with, 183

facial hair, 61, 68, 105, 110
Fairstein, Linda, 232
fantasy, 256–257
of other partners, 257
sexual arousal and, 127
testosterone therapy and, 60–62
Fast, Julius, 183
fat, dietary, 86, 126, 174
fatigue, 80
causes of, 174
in men, 110, 111, 119
testosterone and, 108, 174–175,
179, 200–201
FDA, *see* Food and Drug
Administration
fellatio, 49–50, 71
Fellini, Federico, xxiv
Female Patient, 172
femininity, sexuality *vs.,* 116
feminism, 158
fidelity, marital, 153
financial security, 94, 132
flexibility, exercise for, 193
follicle-stimulating hormone
(FSH), 33
measuring of, 11, 60
Food and Drug Administration
(FDA), 68, 118–119, 145
foreplay, 69, 159
increase in arousal from, 53–54
Fourcroy, Jean, 138–139, 244
Freedman, Rita, 86
freedom, 151
divorce and, 157
intimacy and, 253
middle age and, 181
of widows, 6, 13–14, 18–20,
168

Freud, Sigmund, 221
Friday, Nancy, 239
"Friend Indeed, A," 3
friendship, 94, 132

Gagnon, J. H., 123
Gift from the Sea, A (Lind-
bergh), 181
Goldstein, Irwin, 142
Gordon, Barbara, 112
Great Britain, testosterone
therapy in, 107–108
Greenblatt, Robert, 101, 102,
104–105
Greer, Germaine, xxi–xxv
Grossman, Deborah, 213, 244
gynecologists, 10–11, 138, 244,
248
Gyne-Moistrin, 64, 96, 122

hair, 104
facial, 61, 68, 105, 110
Halverson, Gloria, 244
Harvard Medical School, 105–106
Hayes, Christopher L., 157
HDL cholesterol, 103
headaches, 5, 62, 108, 179
health:
masturbation and, xi, 223
midlife and, 36, 80
sexual desire and, 10, 50, 82
heart attacks, 104
heart disease, *see* cardiovascular
disease
herbs, 76, 134, 173
sexual desire and, 214–215
Heterosexuality (Masters, Johnson,
and Kolodny), 71, 153
Heyn, Dalma, 93
Hickox, Peter, 244
high blood pressure (hypertension), 50, 119, 140–141,
142

Hill, Anita, 232
hirsutism, 61, 68, 104, 105, 110
Hite, Shere, 152
Hite Report, The (Hite), 152
HIV virus, 229
　testing for, 157, 161–162,
　　224–225
homeopathy, 76, 173, 215
hormone levels, testing of, 60, 90,
　95–96
hormone replacement therapy
　　(HRT), x, 11, 26, 65–69
　administration procedures for,
　　66
　benefits of, 67, 134
　hysterectomy and, 66
　intact uterus and, 66, 134
　progesterone in, 66, 67,
　　171–172, 173
　progestin in, 11, 60, 66, 171,
　　173–174
　Quigley's view of, 174
　risks of, 61, 66–68
　side effects of, 61, 65–68
　stress incontinence and, 138
　water retention and, 212
　see also estrogen replacement
　　therapy; testosterone
　　therapy
hormones, 58–77
　body fat and, 95
　follicle-stimulating (FSH), 11,
　　33, 60
　luteinizing (LH), 33
　menopause and, 33, 39, 48,
　　59–63, 92
　sex, 64–65; *see also* estrogen;
　　progesterone; testosterone
　sex and, 62–63, 80, 86, 125
　water retention and, 210, 211,
　　212
hot flashes, 5, 10, 11, 24
　alleviation of, 67, 75–76, 134

body fat and, 95
causes of, 134
in men, 110
House Calls (movie), 184–185
HRT, *see* hormone replacement
　therapy
Human Sexual Response (Masters
　and Johnson), 71, 106
Hunter, Holly, 159
Hutton, Lauren, 205–206
hypertension, *see* high blood
　pressure
hypothalamus, 32, 134
hysterectomy, 23, 34
　hormone replacement therapy
　　and, 66
　sexual desire and, 72–73
Hysterectomy (Cutter), 72–73

illness, 81, 82
　impotence and, 50, 140–141,
　　142, 147–148
　sexual desire and, 50, 97, 119
　see also specific diseases
impotence, 139–146
　cholesterol and, 214
　defined, 140
　doctor visits and, 141–142
　drugs and, 50, 141, 142, 147
　erectile dysfunction vs., 140
　illness and, 50, 140–141, 142,
　　147–148
　incidence of, 141–142
　penile implants and, 144–145
　penile injections and, 145–146
　penile vacuums and, 143–144
　yohimbe bark for, 215
impotence clinics, 79
incontinence, stress, 67, 137–139
infatuation, 184
infections:
　prostate, 119
　urinary-tract, 67, 119

insomnia, 5, 24, 67
  alleviation of, 75–76, 171
  estrogen and, 171
International Menopause Society,
  xxiii, 18
internists, 10, 11
intimacy, 21, 80, 136, 252–259
  body image and, 257–258
  fantasy and, 256–257
  jealousy and, 256
  in lesbian relationships, 27–30
  married couples and, 6, 8,
    54–55, 254–255
  other partners and, 258–259
  sexual sparks and, 254–255
  trust and, 252, 253–254
irritability, 5, 110, 171

Jackson, Glenda, 184
Janus, Cynthia L., 45, 152, 153
Janus, Samuel S., 45, 152, 153
Janus Report on Sexual Behavior,
  45, 49, 114–115, 153,
  218–219
jealousy, 256
Johnson, Virginia E., 56, 71, 106,
  153
Jong, Erica, 225
*Journal of Sex, Education and
  Therapy*, 123
Judd, Howard, 244
Jung, C. G., 250

Kama Sutra, 255
Kaplan, Helen S., 42–43, 55
Kegel, Arnold, 198
Kegel exercises, 138, 198–200
Keitel, Harvey, 159
Kinsey, Alfred C., 56
*Kinsey Institute New Report on
  Sex* (Reinisch), 49, 121,
  220–221, 247

Kinsey Institute of Sex Research,
  152
Kinsey Report, The, 220
kissing, in showers, 186–187
Kolodny, Robert C., 71, 153

Landers, Ann, 217
Lark, Susan, 244
Last Word, The (Buck), 148
Laumann, Edward, 46
LDL cholesterol, 103
Leiblum, Sandra, 243, 248
Leno, Jay, 135
lesbian relationships, 6, 22–30,
  130, 151, 238
Lessing, Doris, 165
Levine, Stephen B., 41–42, 56, 63,
  89, 97, 98, 127, 244, 253
Levinson, Daniel J., 35–36
Lewis, Myrna I., 219
libido, *see* sexual desire
lifespan, extension of, 36, 258–259
Lindbergh, Anne Morrow, 181
Lindsay, Robert, 244
Lisbona, Hanna, 117
literature, erotic, 54, 83, 162,
  187–188
liver, 34
  cholesterol and, 103
  testosterone and, 108, 121
Longcope, Christopher, 104–105
Longevity, 142
long-term relationships:
  boredom in, 202; *see also* sexual
    boredom, avoiding
  changes in, 177–178
  restoring titillation to, 254–255
love, 21, 79, 80, 94, 150–151
  as active goodwill, 131–132,
    133
  body image and, 87
  communication and, 130–133

love (*cont.*)
  in lesbian relationships, 25–28,
    30
  married couples and, 6, 8, 9,
    54–55
  of self, 133, 170, 184, 234, 253
  in sex survey, 132
Love and Sex After 60 (Butler),
    219
lubricants, *see* vaginal
    moisturizers
luteinizing hormone (LH), 33

McClure, Elizabeth, 244
McKinlay, John B., 142
Mademoiselle, sex survey of,
    84–85, 200, 209
Madonna, 194–195
marriage:
  equality in, 158–159
  fidelity in, 153
  open, 155, 237
marriage counselors, 147
*Marriage Made in Heaven, or Too
    Tired for an Affair*
    (Bombeck), 190
married couples, 5–12, 151
  celibacy and, 88
  intimacy and, 6, 8, 54–55,
    254–255
  love and, 6, 8, 9, 54–55
  role reversal and, 160
married women:
  extramarital affairs of, 152–155
  questionnaires and, 38
masculinity, as sexuality, 116–117,
    132, 139
massage, 76, 83, 125, 187, 255
Masters, William H., 56, 71, 106,
    153
masturbation, xi, 44, 69–70,
    217–223
  benefits of, 87–88, 219, 223

children and, 25–26, 219
frequency of, 221
harms of, 220–221
incidence of, 218–219
men and, xxiv, 71, 219
mutual, 224
partnerless people and, 87–88,
    89, 217–223
in sex survey, 84
taboos about, 217–218
Matthau, Walter, 184
Matthews, Roger, 244
Medicott, Joan Avna, 88
men:
  cultural devaluation of, 233
  ego of, 141
  extramarital affairs of, 152,
    153
  fatigue in, 110, 111, 119
  over fifty, sexual intercourse
    and, 70–71
  lack of sexual desire in, 40–41,
    119–120
  masturbation and, xxiv, 71,
    219
  menopause explained to,
    73–75
  menopause of (viropause;
    andropause), 97–98, 110, 111
  midlife transition in, 35–36,
    97–98, 119
  orgasm in, xi, 71, 91
  nurturing self of, 160
  performance anxiety of, 97,
    142, 178
  prostate and, 71, 91, 103, 111,
    119
  quantitative sexual approach
    of, 141
  sexual disease resistance of,
    164
  sexual dysfunction in, 48, 92,
    139–148; *see also* impotence

sexual goals of, 135
sexual peak in, 43, 178
testosterone in, xxiv, 4, 33,
    47–48, 65, 95, 103–106,
    110–111, 160, 178
testosterone therapy for,
    103–106, 111, 120, 121
women's views of, 232–233
menage à trois, 162
menopause, 32–35, 37, 80
    average age at, 32, 96
    consumer seminars on, 74–75
    Gallup poll on, 117–118
    hormones and, 33, 39, 48,
        59–63, 92
    increased vs. decreased desire
        and, 72, 96
    of lesbians, 6, 22–30
    male (viropause; andropause),
        97–98, 110, 111
    partner's knowledge of, 73–75,
        133–135
    premature, 34, 59–62
    surgical, 22–23, 34, 73, 96
    symptoms of, 5, 10–11, 59,
        62–64, 67; *see also* hot
        flashes; night sweats
    uniqueness of, 34, 74
Menopause Management
    (Leiblum), 243
menstruation, menstrual cycle,
        32, 92, 96
    changes in, 10, 11
metabolism, 210, 211
Michael, Robert, 46
Michaels, Stuart, 46
middle age:
    confusion about, vii
    expansion of outer limit of, 36,
        80
    Lindbergh's view of, 181
    sexual behavior in, *see* sex,
        sexual behavior, midlife

midlife transition:
    of men, 35–36, 97–98, 119
    self-esteem and, 184–185
    of women, 36
"Midlife Woman," 2–3
Minnesota, University of, 249
minoxidil cream, 146
Mirabella, xxiv, 227–228
Modern Man in Search of a Soul
    (Jung), 250
monkey testicles,
    transplanting of, 106
Montel Williams Show, The (TV
    program), 79
mood swings, 5, 23
Moore, Carole, 3
*Move On—Adventures in the Real
    World* (Ellerbee), 77
movies:
    sex as portrayed in, viii, 83
    see also videos, erotic; *specific
        movies*
Ms., 158

NAMS, *see* North American
    Menopause Society
National Institute of Aging, 37,
    56, 220
National Institutes of Health
    (NIH), 37, 138, 141
Naus, Peter J., 123, 124
Nemiro, Deborah, 244
nervousness, weight loss and,
    210–211
nervous system, erections and,
    140
New Age workshops, 254
New Joy of Sex, The (Comfort),
    46, 201
Newsweek, 81
Newton, Zachariah, 244
New York Times, The, 103–104,
    107, 141–142, 154, 175, 205

Nielson, Jon, 244
night sweats, 5
   alleviation of, 67, 75–76, 134
   causes of, 134
   communicating about, 133–
      135
   estrogen replacement therapy
      and, 75
   in men, 110
nitric oxide drugs, 146
Nonoxynol 9, 225
North American Menopause
      Society (NAMS), 118, 180,
      243
nutrition, *see* diet

old age, sexual passion in, ix–x, 6,
      12–18
older women:
   constancy of sexual activity in,
      50–52
   relationships between younger
      men and, 20, 155–156
*150 Most-Asked Questions About
      Menopause* (Jacobowitz), 2,
      10, 48, 74, 241, 260
*150 Most-Asked Questions About
      Osteoporosis* (Jacobowitz), 2,
      260
oophorectomy, 34, 66–67
   sexual desire and, 72–73,
      101–102
open marriages, 155, 237
oral sex, 49–50, 69, 71, 84
orgasm, xi, 44, 83, 84, 130
   fantasy and, 127
   masturbation and, 69–70
   in men, xi, 71, 91
   simultaneous, 70, 137
   testosterone therapy and, 61,
      107, 108
   "use it or lose it" edict and, 51
Orgasmatron, 83

Ornish, Dean, 215
osteoporosis, 67, 172, 201
   body fat and, 95
Our Turn (Hayes, Anderson, and
      Blau), 157
ovarian follicle, 33
ovariectomy, *see* oophorectomy
ovaries, 32–34, 64
   brain and, 32–33, 64
   removal of, *see* oophorectomy
   testosterone production in, 33,
      34, 65, 102, 179
overweight, 210, 211–212
   fatigue and, 174
   sexual positions and, 201
oysters, raw, 207

panty liners, 139
papaverine, 146
partners:
   age of, 155–156
   looking for, 89–90, 224
   loss of, 97, 142
   menopause knowledge of,
      73–75, 133–135
   sharing information about
      prior sexual exploits with,
      162
Passages (Sheehy), 36
pelvic muscles, strengthening of,
      138, 198–200
penile implants, 144–145
penile injections, 145–146
penile vacuums, 143–144
penis:
   blood flow to, 140, 142
   Kegel exercises and, 199–200
   see also ejaculation; erection;
      impotence
performance anxiety, 97, 142, 178
phentolamine, 146
pheromones, 182
Phillips, Gerald S., 103

physical appearance, *see* body image
physical examinations, 10, 48, 82, 90, 119
  impotence and, 140–141, 142
physicians, 240–251
  female, 138–139, 243–245
  masturbation as viewed by, 87
  patient communication problems with, 73, 116, 118, 119–120, 241–250
  patient's sexual needs and, 246–247
  testosterone therapy neglected by, 179, 180
  testosterone therapy problems and, 246, 248
  "use it or lose it" edict and, 245–246
  see also specific specialists
Piano, The (film), 159
pituitary gland, 33, 64, 102
Playboy Enterprises, 176
politics, sexual, *see* ethics and politics, sexual
pornography, erotica vs., 122–124
positive attitude, 48
"Postmenopausal Hormone-Replacement Therapy," 37
Prather, Hugh, 57
pregnancy, 33, 96
Premarin, 68, 117, 119
premature menopause, 34, 59–62
Prime Time Live (TV show), Greer interviewed on, xxi–xxii, xxiii
Progest cream, 172
progesterone, 31–33, 64, 72, 179
  in hormone replacement therapy, 66, 67, 171–172, 173
  synthetic, *see* progestin

progestin:
  depression and, 66, 171, 173–174
  estrogen and, 67
  in hormone replacement therapy, 11, 60, 66, 67, 171, 173–174
prostaglandin E, 146
prostate gland:
  cancer of, 103, 111
  infection of, 119
  sexual activity and, 71, 91
  testosterone therapy and, 103, 111
prostitutes, 163, 236–237
puberty, 31, 32
Puritanism, 35, 42

questionnaires, xxii–xxiii, 2, 37–41
  age breakdown of respondents to, 38
  results of, 5, 39, 44–45
Quigley, M. E. Ted, 58–61, 66, 107, 121–122, 173, 244
  on progestin use, 174
  on testosterone therapy, 86–87, 101–104, 108, 109, 111, 118, 172, 201
Quotable Woman, The (Gordon), 112

"Radical Heterosexuality" (Wolf), 158–159
Ramey, Estelle, 48–49, 96, 104, 106, 244
  on anorgasmic women, 56
  on decline of sexual desire, 117–118
  on female body fat, 95
  on frequency of intercourse, 45–46
  on male sex problems, 116

Ramey, Estelle (*cont.*)
  on sexual dangers, 228–229
  on testosterone therapy, 105,
      108, 117, 120–121, 175, 246
  on "use it or lose it"
      philosophy, 91–92
  on women's susceptibility to
      disease, 164
Réage, Pauline, 162
red blood-cell production, 68
Reflections and Maxims (Spinoza),
      128
Reinisch, June M., 37, 46, 49–50,
      71, 81, 244
  on communication, 130, 178,
      230
  on massage, 187
  on masturbation, 220–221
  on penile implants, 144–145
  on sexual encounters, 177
  on testosterone therapy, 121,
      175
  on videos, 176
relaxation therapy, 76
remarriage, lack of interest in,
      157
Replens, 64, 96, 122
reproduction, hormones and, 31,
      33
retirement communities, 236
Risen, Candace B., 230, 232–233,
      244
Roiphe, Katie, 232
role reversal, 160
romance, 79, 83, 94, 132
Rosenblatt, Ellen, 46, 244
Rosenthal, Saul H., 65, 105–106,
      219
runner's high, 194

safer sex, 90
  concern about, 44, 154
      157–158, 161–162, 224–225

  fellatio and, 50
  planning for, 163–164
  see also condoms
satisfaction, *see* emotional
      satisfaction; sexual
      satisfaction
Saunders, Richard M., 123, 124
Schiff, Isaac, 118
Schlaff, William, 244
Schnarch, David M., 84
Scripps Health, 58
seafood, 207, 213
Seasons of a Man's Life, The
      (Levinson), 35–36
*Secrets of Making Love to the
      Same Person Forever* (video),
      176
self-esteem, 48, 133, 169
  body image and, 85, 86
  nutrition and exercise in, 82
  as sex signal, 183–185
  sexual desire and, 41
self-sufficiency, American
      tradition of, 42
sensation, sexual, 166–181
  fatigue and, 174–175
  hormones and, 171–173
  progestin and, 173–174
  recapturing the sexy me and,
      176–177
  videos and, 175–176
sex:
  anatomy of, 31–35
  cultural obsession with,
      78–79
  extramarital, 152–155, 162,
      237–238
  as function of brain, body, and
      hormones, 62–63, 80, 86, 125
  importance of, 185
  lack of frankness about, 79
  oral, 49–50, 69, 71, 84
  safer, *see* safer sex

service or function vs.
  personhood and, 162–163
tantric, 254
work and, 80
sex, sexual behavior, midlife:
  aversion to, 59
  casual, 20, 21, 150, 157–158
  constancy of, 50–52
  embarrassment about, viii, ix,
    35–37
  false image of, viii–ix
  Greer's view of, xxii–xxv
  importance of, 43–44
  of lesbians, 24–28, 30
  role of, 31–57
"Sex After Forty," 3
Sex and the Single Girl (Brown),
  113
sex education, 37, 218, 230, 249
sex hormone–binding globulin,
  111
Sex Information and Education
  Council, 230
Sex Is Not Simple (Levine), 63,
  127, 253
Sex Over Forty (Rosenthal), 65,
  105–106, 219
sex signals, 182–191
  body language as, 182–183
  clothing as, 183, 188–189
  erotic literature as, 187–188
  massage as, 187
  while showering or bathing,
    186–187
  on vacations, 189–190
  walking style as, 186
sex therapists, sex therapy, 79,
  154, 236
  dysfunction as focus of, 84
  locating of, 91, 146–147
sexual abstinence, *see* celibacy
sexual arousal, 113–128
  atmosphere for, 124–125

body image and, 125–126
clothes and, 126
dual hormone therapy and,
  117–118
fantasy and, 127
lack of, 166–167
sexy videos and, 122–124
touching and, 159–160
vaginal moisturizers and, 122
sexual boredom, avoiding, 78–93,
  202
  awakenings and, 78, 82–83
  body image and, 85–87
  celibacy and, 88–89
  frequency of intercourse and,
    92
  lack of desire and, 88–91
  masturbation and, 87–88
  partnerless people and, 87–90
  "use it or lose it" philosophy
    and, 91–92
sexual desire, 94–112
  changes in, 2, 4, 8, 9, 39, 44–45,
    117–118, 177–178
  diet and, 213–214
  estrogen and, 65, 72, 96, 109
  exercise and, 125, 192–202
  hysterectomy and, 72–73
  illness and, 50, 97, 119
  increase vs. decrease in, 72
  increasing of, 94–112
  lack of, 3–4, 5, 39, 40–41, 44,
    52–53, 79–80, 88–91,
    119–120
  nontestosterone factors in, 35,
    40–41, 50–52, 96–97,
    119–120, 197
  oophorectomy and, 72–73,
    101–102
  peaking of, 42–43, 178
  testosterone and, xxiv, 4, 32,
    34–35, 52, 60–62, 64–65, 67,
    72, 73, 86–87, 90–91, 95–96,

sexual desire (*cont.*)
    101–111, 172, 178, 179, 197,
    246
  in young couples, 7–8
sexual dysfunction:
  aging and, 43, 47–49
  defined, 146
sexual encounters, length of, 177
sexual ethics and politics,
  see ethics and politics, sexual
sexual harassment, 232, 233
sexual intercourse, 218
  breaking away from the focus
    on, x–xi, 43–44
  frequency of, 44–47, 55–56, 92,
    255
  Kegel exercises during,
    198–200
  in men over fifty, 70–71
  painful, 2, 3, 4, 9, 11, 48,
    53–54, 63–64, 248
  in sex survey, 84
  simulated, 83
sexually transmitted diseases
    (STDs), 153, 161, 229–230,
    237
  testing for, 157, 161–162, 164
  see also AIDS
sexual needs:
  communicating about, 136–
    137, 155, 178, 230
  doctors and, 246–247
sexual positions, for overweight
    people or people with
    osteoporosis, 201
sexual revolution, viii, 79
sexual satisfaction, 94
  aging stereotype and, 115
  doctors' role and, 247–248
  faking of, 136
  lack of consensus on, 79
sexual surrogates, 163
Shames, Deborah, 202

Sheehy, Gail, 36
Simon, W., 123
single people:
  celibacy among, 88–89
  desire to stay single among,
    157–158
  looking for partners and,
    89–90, 224
  masturbation and, 87–88, 89,
    217–223
  safer sex concerns of, *see* safer
    sex
skin:
  estrogen and, 53, 69
  night sweats and, 134
  "spongy," 85, 86
Slattehaugh, Sharon, 2–3
sleep:
  masturbation and, 88
  orgasm and, 44
  see also insomnia
Sleeper (movie), 83
Slow Waltz in Cedar Bend
    (Waller), 79
Smith, Tom W., 152–153
smoking, 48, 54, 141
*Social Organization of Sexuality,
    The* (Laumann, Michaels,
    and Michael), 46, 153
Society for the Scientific Study of
    Sex, 255
Speaking of Sex (video), 175, 177
spermicides, 225
sphincter muscles, 137, 138
Spinoza, Baruch, 128
Steinem, Gloria, 123–124
Stern, Elizabeth, 244
Stone, Sharon, 183
Story of O, The (Réage), 162
stress, viii, 9, 35, 48, 80, 91, 119,
    175
stress incontinence, 67, 137–139
Studd, John, 107–108

submissiveness, sexual, 158
suicidal tendencies, 24
Summer Before the Dark, The (Lessing), 165
Sunset Boulevard (movie), 169
surgery:
    cosmetic, 86
    for stress incontinence, 138
surgical menopause, 22–23, 34, 73, 96

Tannen, Deborah, 129
tantric sex, 254
teenagers, STDs among, 229
television, sex as portrayed on, viii
tension, 141
    reduction of, 44, 88
testicles:
    eating of, 106
    monkey, transplanting of, 106
Testing Positive (Donovan), 229
testosterone, 31–35, 64–65
    aggression vs. nurturing and, 160
    blood tests and, 60, 90, 95–96
    fatigue and, 108, 174–175, 179, 200–201
    as male hormone, 102–103
    in men, xxiv, 4, 33, 47–48, 65, 95, 103–106, 110–111, 160, 178
    menopausal women and, xxiv, 26, 60–63, 72, 82
    production of, 33, 34, 64, 65, 102–103, 179
    sexual desire and, xxiv, 4, 32, 34–35, 52, 60–62, 64–65, 67, 72, 73, 86–87, 90–91, 95–96, 101–111, 172, 178, 179, 197, 246
    side effects of, 61, 67–68, 103–104, 106–108

testosterone therapy, xxiv, 60–63, 65, 73, 86–87, 90–91, 95, 101–111, 173, 179–180, 246, 248
    administration of, 107, 108–109
    cardiovascular disease and, 103–104, 120–122, 172
    estrogen and, 117–118, 120–121, 172
    fatigue and, 108, 174–175, 179, 200–201
    FDA and, 118–119
    history of, 104–105
    information sources for, 180
    knowledge of, 179–180
    in men, 103–106, 111, 120, 121
    oophorectomy and, 101–102
    orgasm and, 61, 107, 108
    physicians' ignorance about, 179, 180
    risks of, 68, 103–104, 108
    side effects of, 67–68, 103–104, 106–108, 110
    time required for activation of, 109–110
Thomas, Clarence, 232
thyroid gland, 174
thyroxin, 174
touching, sexy, 159–160, 255
tranquilizers, 51
trust, 252, 253–254

urinary-tract infections, 67, 119
urine, leakage of, *see* stress incontinence
urologists:
    female, locating, 138–139
    impotence and, 142
"use it or lose it" edict, 51, 70–71, 91–92, 192, 196, 230, 245–246

uterus, 33, 34
  hormone replacement therapy
    and, 66
  removal of, *see* hysterectomy

vacations, 189–190
vagina, 80
  breast/mouth contact and
    feelings of arousal in, 69
  estrogen cream applied to, 64
  muscles of, 51
  Progest cream and, 172
  susceptibility to diseases and,
    229–230
  tearing of, 63, 164, 230
  thinning and drying of, 2, 4, 5,
    9, 11, 51, 53–54, 63–64, 67,
    91–92, 96, 171, 172, 223
  "use it or lose it" edict and, 51,
    91–92
vaginal moisturizers, 11, 51, 64,
    96, 122
vaginal ultrasound, 174
vanilla beans, 173
vibrators, 70, 136, 137, 222–223
  information sources for,
    222–223
  kinds of, 222
  reliable and helpful, 223
videos, erotic, 54, 59, 122–124,
    136, 162
  how-to, 175–176
  recommendations for, 83,
    175–176, 202
viropause (male menopause,
    andropause), 97–98, 110, 111

Vitamin B$_6$, 212
Vitamin E, 75–76, 134
Vitex (chasteberry), 207, 214
voice:
  deepening of, 68, 104
  as sex signal, 183

walking style, energy and, 186
Waller, Robert James, 79
Waltz, Diane, 88
water, drinking of, 212
water retention, 68, 210–213
weight loss, nervousness and,
    210–211
Weinstein, Sheldon, 244
Wellings, Kaye, 154
widows, 6, 13–21
  freedom of, 6, 13–14, 18–20,
    168
wife abuse, 24–25
Williams, T. Franklin, 138
Wilson, W. C., 123
Wolf, Naomi, 158–159
Women On Top (Friday), 239
Women's International
    Pharmacy, 67, 172, 180

Yaffe, M., 123
yoga, 76, 198
You Just Don't Understand
    (Tannen), 129
younger men, relationships with,
    20, 155–156
younger women, relationships
    with, viii, 156

About the Author

An award-winning medical writer, dynamic lecturer, and a former vice-president at Cleveland's prestigious Mt. Sinai Medical Center, Ruth S. Jacobowitz is author of *150 Most-Asked Questions About Osteoporosis* and *150 Most-Asked Questions About Menopause* and is the co-author of *Managing Your Menopause*. Her lively, informative lectures have taken her all over the country, where with wit, wisdom, and warmth, she educates women about how we age and empowers them to take charge of their health. She has been featured on such television programs as *Today, Donahue, Jerry Springer, CBS Morning Show, America's Talking, Food Television Network, Company, Good Company, Northwest Afternoon, Morning Exchange, People Are Talking,* and *Sonya Live,* as well as on the news and in major newspapers and magazines, National Public Radio, and local radio news and talk shows in the United States and Canada. She is a board member of the National Council on Women's Health, a founding member of the North American Menopause Society, a member of the Jacobs Institute on Women's Health, and a former Midwest chair of the Association of American Colleges Group on Public Affairs. Listed in *Who's Who in American Women* and *Who's Who in the World,* she is also mother of three married daughters and a grandmother of seven. She and her husband, Paul, live in Cleveland, Ohio, and Key Biscayne, Florida.